"In our instant, social criticize or praise churc[...] acquaintance with them. Andy Fitzgerald's socially and theologically informed work is different. He provides an appreciative but also evaluative exploration of Bethel's potential contributions to the wider church. In the process, he also invites us to highlight both Word and Spirit, to bring together the best contributions of evangelical and charismatic realities, and to honor God in Christ by the Spirit."

—**Craig S. Keener**, F. M. and Ada Thompson Professor of Biblical Studies, Asbury Theological Seminary

"Andy Fitzgerald's 'appreciative inquiry' of the ministry of Bethel Church in Redding, California, is a scholarly *tour de force* that seeks to discern the strengths and weaknesses of one of the most influential churches in Northern California. His ethnographic study of its ministry is personal and academic. He doesn't stand outside of the ministry of the church and analyze it from a distance, he participates in it, has dinner with the people who have had an experience of the presence of God at Bethel, and lives in the community that sees the work of Bethel every day. He interviews people who are convinced that something unique is happening at Bethel and those who are skeptical. All this taken together provides a valuable resource in understanding the influence of Bethel Church, creating space for experiencing more of God's supernatural work in the world, and cautions about the possibility of losing the centrality of the gospel of Christ in our search for a supernatural experience of the power of the Spirit."

—**Ron Sanders**, professor and campus minister, Stanford University

"By immersing himself in the phenomenon that is Bethel Church and through the skillful use of world-renowned scholars from a wide variety of disciplines, *A Powerful Presence* offers its readers an expansive, appreciative, critical, fair, and useful portrait of this influential movement. Consequently, Andy Fitzgerald provides contemporary church leaders of any stripe with an exceptional rubric by which they can measure the spiritual vitality and scriptural foundation of any ministry."

—**Bernie A. Van De Walle**, author of *The Heart of the Gospel* and *Rethinking Holiness*

"Evangelicals and secular folks actually share a common thread: faith in what our minds can understand. But Andy pulls on that thread and reveals a need—a desire even—for something more: experiencing God in a real way in the realest parts of our world and lives. In this immersive, appreciative, yet critical look at Bethel, Andy comes back with a way of embodying our faith that is both mind and experience, Scripture and spiritual power."

—**Brian Hui**, lead pastor, Living Stones Christian Church East Bay

"Rooted in a captivating yet nuanced case study of Bethel Church, Fitzgerald offers a tremendous resource for evangelical churches curious about deepening their relationship with the Holy Spirit. Rather than stockpiling resources or clamoring for relevancy, he invites churches to reorient themselves around God's presence."

—**Ryan Russell**, teaching pastor, First Baptist Temple, Texas

A Powerful Presence

A Powerful Presence

An Evangelical Pastor Visits Bethel Church

BY Andy Fitzgerald

FOREWORD BY
David E. Fitch

WIPF *&* STOCK · Eugene, Oregon

A POWERFUL PRESENCE
An Evangelical Pastor Visits Bethel Church

Copyright © 2024 Andy Fitzgerald. All rights reserved. Except for brief
quotations in critical publications or reviews, no part of this book may
be reproduced in any manner without prior written permission from the
publisher. Write: Permissions, Wipf and Stock Publishers, 199 W. 8th Ave.,
Suite 3, Eugene, OR 97401.

Wipf & Stock
An Imprint of Wipf and Stock Publishers
199 W. 8th Ave., Suite 3
Eugene, OR 97401

www.wipfandstock.com

PAPERBACK ISBN: 979-8-3852-3515-5
HARDCOVER ISBN: 979-8-3852-3516-2
EBOOK ISBN: 979-8-3852-3517-9

VERSION NUMBER 12/10/24

Scripture quotations are from the ESV® Bible (The Holy Bible, English
Standard Version®), © 2001 by Crossway, a publishing ministry of Good
News Publishers. Used by permission. All rights reserved.

To Jenny, with love

—Ps 68:35

Contents

Foreword by David E. Fitch | ix
Preface | xiii

1 Introduction: Pastoral Dialogue | 1
2 Bethel Church: Main Observations | 18
3 Faith in Modernity: Our Cultural-Theological Condition | 45
4 Theological Reflection: The Spirit of Life | 62
5 Biblical and Exegetical Analysis: Eschatological Enthusiasm | 82
6 Proposals for the Future: The Pentecostal Angle | 112
7 Conclusion: Word and Spirit | 122

Appendix: Bethel's Responses to Questions and Concerns | 125
Bibliography | 129

Foreword

IN THE LAST TWO decades, Bethel Church, Redding, California, and its School of Supernatural Ministry, have risen to prominence in American Christianity. They have been both lavishly extolled and viciously attacked. Bethel's rise comes largely from its worldwide reputation as a place of the Holy Spirit's movement, accompanied by spectacular healing miracles. Much of the criticism directed its way has been aimed at its theology of the supernatural but also at several of its political positions taken amid a divided nation. The significance of Bethel, and the criticisms weighed against it, suggests it needs some serious theological reflection. More than an academic treatment of Bethel's theology and practice of the supernatural, we need a closer look, one from the inside, where we can we learn from the good and the bad.

It is all too easy these days to assess churches from afar. One look at a website or some "newspaper clippings" we acquire online is all we need these days to disparage a church. It's easy to assess pastors and their ministries from a quick Google search without ever having talked with them. And in so doing, so much is missed. We need to truly understand what God is and is not doing. And this takes listening. This great movement called Bethel is worthy of that kind of attention.

This is what *A Powerful Presence* does. It charts Dr. Fitzgerald's careful listening to Bethel church and its participants. Through interviews, observing the daily practices, spending time

FOREWORD

as one among the people of Bethel, Fitzgerald explores the culture of Bethel like no purist theologian. He then interviews and listens to the mainstream evangelical leaders and churches surrounding Bethel. The dialogue that emerges illumines not only what is happening among people at Bethel but how Bethel is being received or not by evangelical churches, and why or why not.

A Powerful Presence delves deep into both the cultural dynamics that drive Bethel and the churches around it. It explores the ways Bethel Church challenges modern conceptions of the self using the significant scholarship of Charles Taylor and Andrew Root. Fitzgerald probes what is going on here culturally that shapes the ground for Bethel Church to make space for the Spirit, and what perhaps more traditional Evangelicals aren't seeing or understanding.

In all of this, Bethel's theology does not escape scrutiny. Fitzgerald examines the theology of Bethel and how it interacts with surrounding evangelical churches. He uses the insights of Jürgen Moltmann, among others, to explore theologically what is happening on the ground at Bethel in relation to the Spirit. What emerges is not only a deeper understanding of the ways of Bethel's theology but how indeed mainstream Evangelicals clash and or learn from it.

At a time when the evangelical church is facing unparalleled decline, it is my contention that evangelical churches need to listen and understand, and be challenged by the presence of Bethel church in Redding. No one, including mainstream Evangelicals, should blindly accept all we see and hear from Bethel as from God. But God is moving. No one should ignore the flaws of Bethel, where they come from and how they get exposed. This too is part of engaging a church like Bethel that challenges us to live in the Spirit. We need a dialogue that is critical and helps us discern the impact of Bethel and what it means for our future. We need a theological reflection that asks of Bethel and the surrounding engagements, what is the Holy Spirit doing? And how should we as Christians, who come from many other streams of church, join in?

x

FOREWORD

In these times of much church decline and division, Bethel is a challenge to the rest of us. It is time for a radical appraisal of who we are and what we're doing, and Bethel's presence among us provides the occasion for such a task. The evidences of the movement of the Holy Spirit must not be dismissed quickly because of Bethel's perceived excesses or disappointing politics. All of us need to take a deep breath, slow down, dare to read slowly Fitzgerald's engaging work, and ask, how can we make space faithfully for the presence of the Spirit in these most urgent of times?

David E. Fitch

Lindner Chair Evangelical Theology
Northern Seminary

Preface

I THREW THE FIRST Bill Johnson book I ever received in a trash can. It was the only time I had ever discarded a book in such a manner. But these were unprecedented times for my family and me. Our third son, Garrett, had been recently born when we discovered he had Down syndrome. My wife, Jenny, and I had had no idea that our son carried an extra twenty-first chromosome in every cell of his body that would severely impair his physical and mental development. We had no idea, that is, until the attending nurse in the hospital nursery casually suggested it to me. There I was, a proud and loving father, excitedly gazing over my newborn son when the nurse revealed the unexpected news. At that moment it felt like a bomb had exploded. I could not hear anything for the next ten seconds or so. News of Garrett's condition sent shock waves into my world. After collecting myself, I mustered all my courage to deliver the disappointing report to my wife, who was recovering in a nearby room. When we each realized that we both knew of his condition, we cried hard together. We tried to comfort each other the best we could, but neither had much to give. Discovering our newborn child had a genetic disability filled us with a confusing mix of emotions, from excitement to shock to disappointment. On the one hand we were delighted to have Garrett in our lives. On the other hand we did not know what our son's disability meant for us, our family, and, most importantly, for Garrett.

That's where the Bill Johnson book comes in.

PREFACE

My wife and I had a friend who had also recently given birth to a child with Down syndrome. The friend was a fellow believer in Christ, a colleague in ministry, and an Evangelical like us. She sent us the book to encourage us in our journey. She said the book had helped her and her husband after their child was born. I couldn't tell you which Bill Johnson book she gave us, but it didn't matter. Although I appreciated our friend's kindness, as I leafed through its first few pages, I quickly determined that this book *was not for us*. The book's contents seemed fantastical to me, like something out of the "Christian fiction" section of the Christian bookstore. The kind of Christian life Bill Johnson described seemed unimaginable, like Christian speculation masquerading as Christian spirituality.

I had read plenty of books before, especially Christian ones.

I was an evangelical pastor serving in full-time vocational ministry. I was also finishing up my last few courses in a master's in divinity degree, where I studied books on systematic theology, history of doctrine, and biblical languages. I loved books—books were "my thing." And I had never thrown away a book before. I read and kept books even from heterodox groups and cults because I wanted to understand their beliefs better as well as clarify my own. Also, as a pastor, I felt it was my responsibility to defend the church from false teachings. But I made an exception for this Bill Johnson book—throwing it away. I reasoned that I would *not even want to give this book to someone*, fearing that they might read and believe it. I thought throwing away Bill Johnson's book was the pastorally faithful thing to do.

So how does an evangelical pastor who threw away his first Bill Johnson book write a book about Bethel Church?

A few years after Garrett was born, God called my wife and me to plant a new congregation in the San Francisco Bay Area. At the time, I was serving as an associate pastor of a fast-growing, five-hundred-member church, and I was excited to bring the gospel to another area of the Bay Area. Church planting was one of the most thrilling and challenging things we had ever embarked upon. Building a new congregation from the ground up was daunting as

xiv

PREFACE

well as exhilarating. Armed with a giant vision, limited resources, and my own learning curve and insecurities, we stepped out in faith. Planting a new congregation tested our faith and endurance, but God was faithful. He established a small but faithful multigenerational, multiracial evangelical church in the heart of California's Silicon Valley. We were a loving evangelical community devoted to worshipping God and proclaiming the gospel of Jesus Christ.

However, after several years of leading this church, I was confronted with a question that disrupted what had become by then my "well-managed" ministry and life. The question was "If the Holy Spirit stopped showing up at your church, would you know the difference?" The question haunted me. I was a solid Trinitarian, evangelical pastor who believed in the Father, Son, and Holy Spirit. Yet, as I reflected upon the question, I had to admit that if the Holy Spirit had stopped attending our services, I could not tell the difference. The question poked a hole in my thinking and caused a stir in my spirit.

Around this same time, another disruption occurred.

My wife decided to attend a Bethel conference with a friend. My wife's friend was also an Evangelical, and she invited Jenny to join her for a three-day conference in Redding, California. Since our friend lived out of state and we lived only a few hours from Redding, Jenny picked her up from the airport, and they drove north together to Bethel. While on the drive, the unexpected happened: *my wife was physically healed.* Jenny was healed of an ailment that had plagued her for seven years despite numerous visits to the doctor's office and being administered various treatments. My wife's healing was nothing short of a miracle—and it got my attention. We had been in ministry for over twenty years and had never witnessed a divine physical healing before, much less our own.

My wife's healing opened a door in my mind and heart for us to explore Bethel more. I started reading Bill Johnson's books and attended a conference where he and other charismatic leaders spoke. At the conference, I witnessed healings, miracles, and unusual "manifestations," such as people shaking, falling, and laughing. It was all new to me. I also further acquainted myself with the person and work of the Holy Spirit through authors such as Gordon Fee, John V. Taylor, and James E. Loder.

After a few years of exploration, my wife and I made a bold move. We felt God's call to move our family (four children by this time) to Redding and check out Bethel Church more. The move allowed me to finish my doctoral work in contextual theology. The nature of contextual theology is to go personally or incarnationally to see how God is at work in a particular location. Therefore, I thought moving to Redding was a fitting thing to do. I wanted to see firsthand how God was moving (or not) at Bethel Church. Here I was, an evangelical pastor visiting a charismatic church like Bethel.

The following book is a product of my time at Bethel. As the reader will see, this book is not an apologetic or criticism of Bethel but a pastoral reflection on one congregation's life in Christ and its understanding and use of supernatural power. God's supernatural power is at the heart of the gospel and Christ's kingdom (1 Thess 1:5; Rom 1:16; 1 Cor 4:20). Divine power is also an essential aspect of the church's life in Christ and its mission to the world (Matt 10:8; 1 Cor 2:4, 2 Tim 1:7). As Charles Spurgeon astutely observed, "Miracles of grace must be the seals of our ministry; who can bestow them but the Spirit of God?" Therefore, I wanted to know how Bethel Church understood and practiced supernatural power and how spiritual leadership was administered in such an environment. I observed and interviewed people and heard their accounts of God's otherworldly action. Consistent with the practice of contextual theology, I also engaged with Bethel's structures and frameworks that shape members' perceptions of events. My experience at Bethel was personally and vocationally enriching. My hope here is to put this experience in service to God and his kingdom to build up Christ's church. As I explore how God was at work at Bethel culturally and theologically, I intend for readers to discern how God is or can be a powerful presence in their context.

Chapter 1

Introduction: Pastoral Dialogue

True contextualization accords the gospel its rightful primacy, its power to penetrate every culture and to speak within each culture, in its own speech and symbol, the word which is both No and Yes, both judgment and grace.—Lesslie Newbigin, *The Gospel in a Pluralist Society*

IN 2017, REBECCA CUPP was a seventy-seven-year-old wife and grandmother living in Southern California with congestive heart failure. Rebecca's precarious condition was the result of a heart attack she had suffered five years earlier, leaving one chamber of her heart unresponsive. Rebecca was constantly tired, out of breath, and restricted to living from a chair. She struggled even to keep pace with her husband, Eric, while shopping at the grocery store or leisurely walking around the neighborhood. Rebecca was required to carry with her an inhaler of nitroglycerine in case her breathing became too difficult. Despairing of life, Rebecca cried out to God to "take her home" if he would not heal her. Rebecca made this plea from her born-again faith in Christ and faithful attendance at her local church. Neither Rebecca nor her doctors had any hope for a cure.

Then, one day, Rebecca attended a conference at Bethel Church. The conference was called "Healing and Impartation," and Randy Clark, a healing evangelist, was its keynote speaker. At the conference, with over one thousand people gathered, Randy Clark spoke from God's word and shared testimonies of God's healing power. At the close of his message, Clark declared, "Somebody here needs a new heart." The healing evangelist then invited audience members to stand up if they believed the "word of knowledge" applied to them. Rebecca quickly rose from her seat, believing the Lord had identified her and her condition. As Rebecca stood, what she describes as "an electric shock bolt" hit her square in the chest. Rebecca lost control of her body and fell to the floor with "electricity" pulsating throughout her. She says she would have collapsed onto the seat in front of her if Eric and a stranger sitting next to her had not held her up. After several moments "under the power of God," Rebecca regained consciousness. When she did, Rebecca knew she had been healed.

Rebecca and the other conferees who believed they had been healed were invited to the platform stage to share their testimonies of healing. Once there, Randy Clark interviewed Rebecca to learn of her previous health condition and testify to the healing. Clark asked Rebecca, "What's one thing you couldn't do before?" Rebecca shared about being constantly tired, out of breath, and unable to walk with her husband. Clark then asked Rebecca, "Okay. Well, what can you do now?" Immediately the seventy-seven-year-old began running around the stage and up and down the platform stairs. As Rebecca ran, an enormous roar erupted from the conference crowd. At first, Rebecca was startled by the crowd's sound, but she soon realized *they were cheering for her*. Rebecca left the conference and returned to Southern California, knowing God had healed her heart.

Once returning home, Rebecca reported her healing to her cardiologist, who called her in for a checkup. The cardiologist, being skeptical yet professional, instructed Rebecca to undergo an echocardiogram to test the condition of her heart. After receiving the test results, the doctor informed Rebecca that her heart

INTRODUCTION: PASTORAL DIALOGUE

was in excellent shape. Indeed, Rebecca's heart was so healthy that the doctor told her humorously, "You're ready to live to 150 [years old]!" The doctor explained that Rebecca's ejection fraction, which measures the amount of blood the heart pumps with each contraction, was 70 percent higher than before. The test verified what Rebecca and Eric believed: God had healed her heart. Rebecca and Eric have kept the echocardiogram report with them to this day as proof of her divine healing.[1]

Because of her healing miracle, Rebecca and Eric packed up their RV and moved to Redding, California. They said they wanted to be a part of the dynamic power evident at Bethel Church. Today, Rebecca and Eric are active Bethel members, participating in Sunday worship services, small group ministry, and a healing ministry called the healing rooms.

Bethel Church, Redding, California

Stories like Rebecca's are remarkable but not uncommon at Bethel Church in Redding, California. Redding is not known as a destination location within the Golden State. By California standards, it is an average-sized city situated off the I-5 interstate in the upper corridor of Northern California. Redding is 300 miles north of San Francisco and 125 miles south of the California/Oregon border. The nearest large city to Redding is the state's capitol, Sacramento, which is 160 miles southeast. Redding operates like a large city among rural towns, populated with sprawling hills, nearby 14,000-foot mountains, and fertile lakes. As a 9,000+ member congregation, Bethel is a behemoth within Redding. Its membership is roughly 10 percent of the city.[2] The next largest church is a traditional evangelical congregation of about 2,400 members.

---

1. Rebecca and Eric recorded their cardiologist's visit on their cellphone, which I watched during my interview with them.

2. According to the 2022 U.S. Census Bureau statistics, approximately 90,000 people live in Redding. See United States Census Bureau, Redding City, California, "2020 Population," https://www.census.gov/quickfacts/fact/table/reddingcitycalifornia/POP010220.

Bethel Church was launched in 1952 and affiliated with the Assemblies of God in 1954.[3] In the 1980s, Bethel experienced considerable growth, increasing to 2,200 members and building a 46,000-square-foot facility on seventy-one acres of land. However, Bethel's meteoric rise to global prominence came under its current leader, Bill Johnson. Interestingly, Bill Johnson grew up at Bethel Church under the leadership of his late father, M. Earl Johnson. However, the younger Johnson did not inherit Bethel's mantle directly from his father.[4] Bill Johnson first served for seventeen years at another Assemblies of God church nearby in Weaverville, California. During his time in Weaverville, Johnson was exposed to John Wimber and the Vineyard movement and Wimber's "signs and wonders" ministry. In the 1980s, Wimber advanced a third-wave Pentecostalism emphasizing signs, wonders, and miracles.[5] Wimber also pioneered a form of "power evangelism" where the supernatural spiritual gifts were directed toward evangelism and church growth.[6] After witnessing Wimber's "signs and wonders" ministry, Bill Johnson said he wanted "the more of God." Bill Johnson and his late wife, Beni Johnson, were also significantly influenced by the Toronto Airport Vineyard revival in 1995.[7] Also known as the "Father's Blessing," the Toronto outpouring was characterized by increased awareness of God's love, extraordinary miracles, and ecstatic manifestations

---

3. Jones, "Inside the Popular, Controversial," para. 6.

4. The following biographical information on Bill Johnson comes from various sermons and presentations heard at Bethel Church and BSSM.

5. On the difference between Pentecostals and charismatics, see Burgess and Van der Maas, *New International Dictionary*. They write that it is a helpful oversimplification, but "*pentecostals* refers to those participating in classical pentecostal denominations, such as the Assemblies of God, the Church of God (Cleveland, TN), the Church of God in Christ, the United Pentecostal Church, and the International Church of the Foursquare Gospel. *Charismatics*, on the other hand, refer to persons outside these classical pentecostal denominations but with connection to mainline denominations" (xxi).

6. Springer and Wimber, *Power Evangelism*.

7. Johnson, *When Heaven Invades Earth*, 97.

INTRODUCTION: PASTORAL DIALOGUE

such as laughter, crying, falling, and fainting.[8] Bill and Beni Johnson said that this move of God touched them deeply. When Bill Johnson was called to lead Bethel Church in 1996, he brought third-wave revivalism to a classical Pentecostal church. And not every Bethel member was pleased. Over 1,000 members left the church during Johnson's first year. They were uncomfortable with Johnson's emphasis on modern-day healings, deliverances, signs, wonders, and miracles. Soon after the mass exodus, Bethel Church disaffiliated with the Assemblies of God and became independent. But for those Bethel members who remained and endured Johnson's early tumultuous years, they witnessed a local congregation grow into a global phenomenon.

Today Bethel boasts over 9,000 members, 800 staff, and five weekend worship services. Bethel is also home to several schools. For example, Bethel School of Supernatural Ministry (BSSM) is its flagship school, enrolling 1,200 "future revivalists" from over forty nations annually.[9] Bethel houses K–12 primary and secondary schools. Bethel School of Technology is a one-year online computer coding school. Bethel Conservatory of the Arts seeks to equip students for service in the arts and entertainment industry. In addition to its schools, Bethel hosts several annual conferences that attract thousands. These conferences include "Healing and Impartation," "Heaven Come," and "Prophetic Conference." Bethel is also the home of several niche ministries. For example, Bethel Music is a widely popular worship and music ministry.[10] Bethel Global Outreach is the congregation's overseas mission arm. Global Response provides relief and support to those who are poor or under-resourced. Heaven in Business equips

---

8. Poloma, "Toronto Blessing."

9. Bethel Church is the nation's largest enroller of international vocational students. See "M-1 Schools," listings 2 and 3, in U.S. Immigrations and Customs Enforcement, *SEVIS by the Numbers*, 16.

10. According to a verbal report on Feb. 28, 2023, during the Bethel Church annual business meeting, Bethel Music produced four of the top ten Christian worship songs in the world. Bethel Music's song "The Goodness of God" won the 2023 Dove Song of the Year Award. See https://godtv.com/goodness-of-god-won-as-the-song-of-the-year-during-the-gma-dove-awards/.

business leaders with "kingdom principles" for the marketplace. The Changed Movement helps individuals from an LGBTQ+ background find hope, healing, and wholeness.[11] Bethel is also undertaking a new land and facilities project to accommodate their explosive growth. The new campus, referred to as a "global apostolic center," will be the home of a 2,600-seat sanctuary on fifty-eight acres of land.[12] The project will cost an estimated 93 million dollars, and Bethel intends to pay for it in cash.

Focus of the Book

I was interested in Bethel Church as a North American neo-charismatic church practicing supernatural faith in late modernity.[13] Dallas Willard understands supernatural ministry as involving "extraordinary events or powerful effects not easily attributable, if attributable at all, to merely natural causes."[14] Today's modern and secular West is often skeptical of supernatural occurrences because it sees the world as a closed universe of natural laws. Nonetheless, within this modern landscape, Bethel promotes a supernatural faith of signs, wonders, healings, and miracles. And its message is catching on. Bethel is a part of the larger global charismatic/Pentecostal movement, an outgrowth of nineteenth-century Wesleyan-Holiness movements. Sociologist Peter Berger calls twentieth-century Pentecostalism the "most explosively

11. See http://www.changedmovement.com/changed-on-change, s.v. "About Us."

12. "Arise and Build" (Bethel Church brochure; no further publication information available).

13. Burgess and Van der Maas define *neo-charismatics* as "a catch-all category that comprises 18,810 independent, postdenominational denominations and groups that cannot be classified as either pentecostal or charismatic but share a common emphasis on the Holy Spirit, spiritual gifts, pentecostal-like experiences (not pentecostal terminology), signs and wonders, and power encounters. In virtually every other way, however, they are as diverse as the world's culture they represent" (*New International Dictionary*, xx). The Vineyard Christian Fellowship is an example of a neo-charismatic communion.

14. Willard, *Hearing God*, 49.

INTRODUCTION: PASTORAL DIALOGUE

growing movement in the history of religion."[15] After more than a century of Pentecostalism, the world's religious landscape has changed significantly. Pentecostal faith and practice influence every aspect of the church worldwide. Stanley Burgess and Eduard van der Mass observe,

> The 20th century witnessed the emergence and phenomenal growth of the pentecostal, charismatic, and neocharismatic movements. These three waves of pentecostalism, which constitute one of Christianity's greatest renewals, have impacted every segment of the church in virtually all countries of the world with new vitality and fervor.[16]

I was interested in Bethel Church as a local expression of charismatic/Pentecostal Christianity in today's modern Western landscape.

In exploring Bethel Church, I was also interested in how traditional Evangelicals in Redding understood and related to the charismatic megachurch. I had my own questions concerning Bethel, but I also wanted to hear from Evangelicals who lived nearby. Many Evangelicals are exposed to Bethel through media such as YouTube, books, publications, and social media. While considering these voices, I also wanted to interact with those who lived locally, presuming they had more *direct contact* with the charismatic church.

By exploring Bethel and listening to Redding evangelical leaders, I was interested in the intersection between neo-charismatic and evangelical faith, especially considering what scholar Andrew Root calls the church's current "crisis of decline."[17] Root argues that many churches in North America today feel the tide of secularism enclosing. This modern enclosure is felt most acutely with declining denominations, decreased church membership, fewer resources, and waning social influence. Over the last hundred years,

15. Peter Berger, *The Explosive Growth of Pentecostalism*, Berkley Center, accessed June 6, 2023, https://www.youtube.com/watch?v=0tGXBuYXpwk/.

16. Burgess and Van der Maas, *New International Dictionary*, xvii.

17. Root, *Churches and the Crisis*.

the Christian church has been increasingly marginalized in the American imagination, resulting in many church leaders feeling displaced. News reports abound of how fewer Americans regularly attend church today. Specifically, much attention has been given to the rise of the "Nones" in America.[18] The Nones represent a younger generation of Americans who do not identify with any religious community but consider themselves "religiously unaffiliated."[19] Another group of Americans that has caught the eye of observers and church leaders is the "Dones."[20] The Dones represent Americans who used to attend church regularly but no longer do so for various reasons. The rise of the Dones has been called one of the most significant shifts in American church history![21] With the rise of the Nones and Dones, many church leaders are flummoxed on how to reach them. Many churches feel like they are playing on the losing team with time on the clock running out.

While evangelical churches struggle to attract new members, Pentecostal and charismatic congregations seem to be growing.[22] Some Evangelicals see their charismatic cohorts as "competitors," contending for what they consider legitimate forms of biblical Christianity. Some Evangelicals could be tempted to look at the growth and influence of their charismatic colleagues with righteous jealousy or unholy fear.

18. White, *Rise of the Nones*; Bush and Wason, *Millennials and the Mission*.

19. According to the American Religious Identification Survey, the Nones grew from 8 percent of the U.S. population in 1990 to 15 percent in 2008. See Kosmin et al., *American Nones*.

20. See Schultz, "Rise of the Dones."

21. Authors Jim Davis, Michael Graham, and Ryan Burge say, "We are currently in the middle of the largest and fastest religious shift in the history of [America]." Drawing from the research of Burge, they conclude that more Americans have left the church in the last twenty-five years than those who joined during the First and Second Great Awakenings and the Billy Graham Crusades *combined* (Davis et al., *Great Dechurching*, 5).

22. Also drawing from the research of Burge, Ed Stetzer says that from 2005 to 2019, the Southern Baptists in America were down in membership by 11 percent, and the United Methodists were down by 19 percent. However, during this same time, the Assemblies of God grew 16 percent to nearly 3.3 million members (Stetzer, "Pentecostals"). Also see Nieuwhof, "5 Reasons Charismatic Churches."

INTRODUCTION: PASTORAL DIALOGUE

As a pastor and church planter, I relate to these sentiments. Every pastor I know wants to reach people with the gospel. I wondered how Redding Evangelicals understood and responded to Bethel. Understanding the dynamic between Bethel Church and Redding evangelical congregations could have implications for broader Christian faith, practice, and mission in America.

Ethnography

I spent four months at Bethel Church listening to the church ethnographically. Ethnography is a discipline associated with sociology, but it can be applied to congregations. Ethnographic practice can lead to pastoral listening and care with the hope of prophetic leadership. Mary Clark Moschella defines ethnography as "a way of immersing yourself in the life of a people in order to learn something about them and from them."[23] Ethnography as a pastoral practice opens listeners to how people practice their faith. Ethnography draws from narrative models of theology and praxis that "recognize the importance of storytelling as a hallmark of human experience."[24] I was interested in the personal experiences of Bethel members and their stories of supernatural power—in addition to their beliefs, doctrines, and practices. I aimed to obtain qualitative, not quantitative, data about the church. Many people associate sociological inquiry with quantitative research, which can involve collecting and analyzing data, applying objective empirical investigations, and employing mathematical measurements. Qualitative research is different. Qualitative analysis consists in exploring the stories, experiences, imaginations, forces, and forms of a people (or, in this case, a congregation). I intended to listen to Bethel members' experiences, stories, and practices rather than measure their responses. I felt that by listening to Bethel members, I would gain insight into the church's spirit, soul, and imagination. In researching Bethel, I noticed that some books and articles about

23. Moschella, *Ethnography as Pastoral Practice*, 4.
24. Moschella, *Ethnography as Pastoral Practice*, 5.

the church rarely included the personal accounts of current Bethel members. Indeed, I was uncertain if some authors had even visited the church. I felt that by interacting personally with and listening to Bethel members, I would gain a deeper and richer understanding of Bethel's appeal, character, and practices.

Therefore, as part of the ethnographical process, I immersed myself in Bethel Church. I was a participant observer and interviewer at the congregation. As a participant observer, my family and I attended weekly worship services, ministry events, and informal social gatherings. I met and observed people in their natural setting of religious community life. I spoke with Bethel members, participated in formal and informal conversations, made observations, and took ethnographic field notes. I participated daily in Bethel Church, interacting with their members, leaders, structures, and frameworks. My involvement occurred in various settings. For example, on some occasions, my family and I were guests of Bethel members in their homes. On other occasions, Bethel members were guests in our home. For instance, I met Rebecca and Eric Cupp and heard their story of miraculous healing through an informal social gathering at our house. I participated in "revival groups" and took enrichment classes like "Revival History."

I also enrolled in Bethel's "supernatural" ministry school, BSSM. BSSM is an unaccredited adult ministry school to which one must apply and be accepted. BSSM students can enroll for up to one to three years. BSSM graduates do not receive a diploma but a "certificate of completion." By enrolling in BSSM, I felt I could gain an insider's view of how Bethel prepares what they consider "future revivalists." My involvement at BSSM allowed me *daily* exposure to Bethel's beliefs and practices. I did not feel that being a participant observer at the church and school imbued me with a "hidden agenda." Indeed, several BSSM pastors and leaders knew of my interest in the church and welcomed my research nonetheless. As a large church often in the public eye— and viewed as controversial—they were especially accommodating to, if not interested in, in my work.

INTRODUCTION: PASTORAL DIALOGUE

In addition to my role as a participant observer, I sat down with Bethel members for intensive interviews. During the interviews, I asked Bethel members specific questions regarding their experiences of the church and supernatural power. For example, when I spoke with Rebecca and Eric Cupp, listening to them and asking them follow-up questions was helpful. For my interviews, I drew from a broad range of people representing diverse life experiences. I conducted intensive interviews with Bethel's general congregation and BSSM students. I spoke with young adults, adults, males, females, singles, and married people with children. I interviewed people who were Afro-Latino, of European descent, and from Asia. However, most of the interviewees were Caucasian Americans. I did not seek a "representative sampling" as my purposes were qualitative, not quantitative. I contacted interviewees through personal relationships and recommendations. Only three interviewees were explicitly selected due to their experiences of supernatural healing. They were Rebecca Cupp, Kevin (a Bethel pastor), and a friend visiting from England (mentioned in chapter 2). I was interested in the nature and events surrounding their healing events. The other Bethel interviewees were selected due to other factors, such as race, gender, or the convenience of knowing them personally. One interviewee, Becky, was chosen because of her extensive knowledge of Bethel's history. Becky was introduced to me by a Bethel pastor, who described her as "the resident historian of the church." Kevin was the only Bethel pastor I officially interviewed. I also interviewed one *former* Bethel attendee to gain the perspective of someone who had left the church. The interviews lasted thirty minutes to one and a half hours, with an average of forty-five minutes. During the interviews, I asked about their religious history, reasons for attending the church, and experiences of God's supernatural power. I also inquired about any negative experiences associated with Bethel and their practice of supernatural power. For this book, I changed the names of all interviewees to protect anonymity and ensure honest reporting. The only Bethel members identified by name are leaders Bill and Beni Johnson and Kris Vallotton.

A POWERFUL PRESENCE

Redding Evangelical Leaders

In addition to interviewing Bethel members, I talked with numerous Redding evangelical pastors and church leaders about Bethel. These leaders represented several evangelical churches in town, reflecting a range of evangelical expressions, from conservative to charismatic. I chose leaders and churches I considered my evangelical colleagues in vocational ministry. All leaders and their representative churches affirmed traditional evangelical faith, such as the necessity of personal faith in Christ for salvation, the mandate to share the gospel of Christ, Scripture as the authoritative word of God, and the centrality of Christ's crucifixion.[25] As examples of the range of evangelical expression, one church leader described himself as "John MacArthur without the edge." Another pastor considered himself "charismatic" but profoundly shaped by authors not typically associated with Pentecostalism, such as Dallas Willard, Eugene Peterson, and Erwin McManus. I spoke with senior pastors, associate pastors, and elder/board members to hear their perspectives on their churches and Bethel. One qualification I placed was that I interviewed only those who believed that spiritual gifts were in operation today. In other words, I interviewed only Christian leaders who were continuationists, not cessationists, concerning spiritual gifts. Wayne Grudem defines *cessationism* as the belief "that certain miraculous spiritual gifts ceased long ago, when the apostles died and Scripture was complete."[26] I reasoned that by speaking with cessationists, an entirely different conversation would occur—on the legitimacy of the supernatural gifts today.

25. I use "evangelical" here as distinct but related to Pentecostalism and charismatic Christianity. I define "evangelical" following D. W. Bebbington's four characteristics: conversionism, activism, biblicism, and crucicentrism (*Evangelicals in Modern Britain*, 2–17). Concerning the relationship between charismatics and Evangelicals, following Bebbington, I see charismatics as a renewal movement within traditional Evangelicalism. Bebbington states, "The charismatic upsurge represented another mutation in the Protestant tradition comparable to that which created Evangelicalism in the eighteenth century and that which modified it in the nineteenth. Once more a fresh cultural current impinged on popular religion" (248).

26. Grudem, *Systematic Theology*, 1031.

12

INTRODUCTION: PASTORAL DIALOGUE

Therefore, for this book, I spoke with Evangelicals who believed in the contemporary use of all the spiritual gifts, including the "supernatural" ones like healing, miracles, signs, and wonders.

My Story

In exploring Bethel, I did not seek to understand the church from a purely "objective" point of view, at least in the modern sense. I understood that my perspective was informed by my life, faith, and practices and that I carry these experiences into my conversations. *Reflexivity* is a term sociologists use to describe one's role in the research and its influence on the results.[27] As mentioned, I came to Bethel as an evangelical pastor interested in neo-charismatic faith and supernatural practice in a modern Western context—and its intersection with traditional Evangelicalism. My story entails coming to personal faith in Christ while a nineteen-year-old undergraduate at a large Midwestern university. After a Cru staff member (formerly Campus Crusade for Christ) shared the gospel with me on the back of an *Athletes in Action* magazine, I knew I needed *and wanted* Christ in my life. I became heavily involved with the Cru and Navigators fellowships on campus. I also weekly attended a local "Bible church" where all of the pastoral staff were graduates of Dallas Theological Seminary. Upon graduation, I joined Cru staff, serving on two university campuses for fourteen years. I spent the last ten years as a Cru campus director at the University of California at Berkeley. At Berkeley, I loved the challenge of taking the gospel to students and faculty who often considered Christianity irrelevant, ignorant, or, at worst, outright oppressive. After getting married and having our first three (of four) children, I accepted a position as an associate pastor at a five-hundred-person Evangelical Covenant church in the San Francisco Bay Area. After serving this congregation for three years, they tapped me to launch a new congregation in another area of the Bay Area. By God's grace, my wife and I, along with a

27. Moschella, *Ethnography as Pastoral Practice*, 32.

team of fifteen, planted a multiracial congregation in an economically diverse area of San Jose. I led this church for fourteen years until leaving to complete my doctoral studies.

As mentioned, I am an evangelical pastor whose faith and practice have been primarily shaped by evangelical ministries, churches, and institutions. In addition to completing a master of divinity degree (Fuller Seminary), I also completed a doctorate of ministry degree emphasizing contextual theology (Northern Seminary). *Contextual theology* seeks to understand how God is at work in new settings.[28] Contextual theology is not cultural relativism or determinism but a missiological focus involving the gospel in particular contexts.[29] Contextual theology takes seriously the relationships among three realities: gospel, church, and culture. The gospel is the "good news" of the arrival of God's kingdom in Jesus Christ (Mark 1:15; Matt 10:7; Luke 21:31). James Dunn says the gospel "denotes the manifest rule of God whose intervention will bring an end the history of this world as we know it and its judgment."[30] The *church* is the redeemed people of God, chosen to inhabit, exhibit, and announce the good news to the world's principalities in the power of the Spirit. *Culture* involves a people's historical, religious, political, geographical, and relational world.[31] Culture consists of how people live and relate to one another and the systems by which they operate. As such, contextual theology involves engaging with peoples' frameworks, not just their cultural artifacts and expressions. When the gospel, church, and culture converge in pastoral conversation, the contextual theologian seeks to discern the work of God in new times and locations. The practice of contextual theology is essential to the church's mission, for Christ intends his message to be translated into new situations (*transmission*). Missiologist Andrew Walls says gospel transmission

28. Bevans, *Models of Contextual Theology*, 1.

29. Richard Hays understands contextual theology as "imaginative analogies between the stories told in the texts [of Scripture] and the story lived out by the community in a very different historical setting" (*Moral Vision*, 298).

30. Dunn, *Unity and Diversity*, 13.

31. Brown, *Scripture as Communication*, 191.

INTRODUCTION: PASTORAL DIALOGUE

enriches the church's identity and call. He writes, "It is a delightful paradox that the more Christ is translated into the various thought forms and life systems which form our various national identities, the richer all of us will be in our common Christian identity."[32] My contextuality affirms the vision of the *missio Dei*, which holds that God is at work in the world—even ahead of the church—to unite all things in Christ (Eph 1:10). When the contextual theologian considers the three factors of gospel, church, and context in the wisdom of the Spirit, the hope is to bring forth "a timely word" for the church in its season (Prov 15:23).

Appreciative Inquiry

My pastoral approach to discerning God's action at Bethel draws from Marc Lau Branson's recommendation of "appreciative inquiry." Branson describes appreciative inquiry as more than a research method or a strategy for change but a way to bring the narratives of a congregation "into conversations with the biblical and historical narratives of our faith."[33] Appreciative inquiry is not a "positivist approach" to problem-solving or congregational change (where an organization is studied "objectively"). Such positivist approaches seek to explore congregations "scientifically" using research methods, closed questionnaires, structured interviews, experiments, and uncovering and measuring behavior patterns. The thesis of appreciative inquiry holds

> that an organization, such as a church, can be recreated by its conversations. And if that new creation is to feature the most life-giving forces and forms possible, then the conversations must be shaped by appreciative questions.[34]

Appreciative inquiry explores a congregation's "most life-giving forces and forms" by asking *appreciative questions*. Appreciative

32. Walls, *Missionary Movement*, 54.

33. Branson, *Memories, Hopes, and Conversations*, 21.

34. Branson, *Memories, Hopes, and Conversations*, xvii.

A POWERFUL PRESENCE

inquiry seeks questions such as: How does the gospel nourish members' lives? How were God's actions highlighted and glorified in this place? What makes this congregation come alive in Christ and display the power and fruit of the Spirit? What propels this congregation toward faithful mission? What practices, beliefs, and frameworks led to spiritual renewal and congregational change? In short, appreciative inquiry helps congregations explore, discern, imagine, and experiment with God for a more positive future.[35]

Therefore, I approached Bethel Church by seeking its strengths and asking appreciative questions rather than strictly from the standpoint of problem-solving or *critique*. When pastors approach congregations through the lens of problem-solving or criticism, a congregation's deficits determine what one can see, hear, or otherwise observe. Therefore, I inquired about the life-giving forces and forms at Bethel and how the gospel enriched lives there. Nonetheless, I still expected instances of dissonance and critique to emerge. These occasions of dissonance and critique are essential in discerning God's action in a location, and I note them in the following chapters.[36]

Summary

In sum, my approach to Bethel Church in this book is pastoral dialogue. Pastoral dialogue is not a one-way street but is conducted with a profound openness to context and the people living there. It involves noncoercive conversations as both parties listen to and are shaped by one another. However, through respectful dialogue, sometimes a "counterpoint" from the outside can stimulate people to do their own theological thinking. The central question I explore is: *How does Bethel Church understand and practice supernatural power?* Through attentive listening, asking questions, and being an insider, I hoped to understand and discern the meanings of supernatural power at Bethel and reflect upon its human, social,

35. Branson, *Memories, Hopes, and Conversations*, 21.

36. I include an appendix of some of Bethel's responses to its positions and practices.

INTRODUCTION: PASTORAL DIALOGUE

and theological significance. My hope in this journey is for new insights, learnings, and pathways to emerge for the church, its identity, and its mission in late modernity.

Chapter 2

Bethel Church: Main Observations

The Presence of God is the central fact of Christianity. At the heart of the Christian message is God Himself waiting for His redeemed children to push in to conscious awareness of His Presence.—A. W. Tozer, *The Pursuit of God*

WHEN I FIRST ARRIVED at Bethel, I wondered how the church practiced charismatic faith and supernatural power. For example, I was curious to how they practiced the gifts of healing, words of knowledge, and prophecy and what kind of effect these practices had, if any. As an Evangelical, I had never been involved in a "supernatural" church. As a church leader, I was interested in how Bethel leaders trained and equipped members to serve in these otherworldly gifts. I also wondered how ecstatic physical manifestations such as shaking, falling, and excessive crying or laughing operated. Were they real? Were they contrived? I had never personally experienced these manifestations (nor have I since visiting Bethel).

In my conversations with Redding evangelical leaders, I heard a range of sentiments regarding Bethel. Redding church leaders expressed positive, neutral, and negative opinions about the church. For example, one Redding church leader, who described him and his church as "charismatic," said they often partnered with Bethel in ministry. However, he differed from Bethel in saying, "We're charismatic but not in the classical Pentecostal kind of way. . . . There's a lot of weird things we don't allow, like blowing shofars." Other Redding leaders were neutral or indifferent toward Bethel. For example, one Redding lead pastor expressed concerns about Bethel's apparent victorious end-time eschatology and use of the Passion Translation, which he considered not a Bible translation but a paraphrase. Another Redding lead pastor said that his congregation did not think about Bethel much. However, he saw a place for Bethel to help them learn to use the spiritual gifts of healing, prophecy, and words of knowledge. And still other Redding church leaders viewed Bethel negatively. For example, one lead pastor said about Bethel, "They know the Holy Spirit, they know emotions, [but] they don't know the saving work of Jesus Christ . . . " He continued, "They are stuck on Holy Spirit, Holy Spirit, Holy Spirit." "They have a misplaced center of the circle, and it is not 'Christ crucified . . . It is 'supernatural ministry, supernatural manifestations." When asked about the stories of God's supernatural power that come from Bethel, he described them as analogous to slices of a pizza pie. He said, "Some of the things that they do are from God, some are of human origin, and some are of the devil."

Main Observations

Considering these perspectives of Redding evangelical leaders and my own experiences and interviews, I had three main observations concerning Bethel Church and its experience of supernatural power. They are that Bethel Church (1) practiced a presence-centered spirituality, (2) empowered ministry through spiritual gifts, and (3) viewed revival as its imagination and ethos. I explore each observation below.

A POWERFUL PRESENCE

Presence-Centered Spirituality[1]

The first observation is that Bethel Church practiced a presence-centered spirituality. Bethel's central focus and locus of worship, ministry, and community life was the desire for God's manifest presence. From their prayer chapel at the center of campus to "encounter rooms" where people "soaked" in God's presence to their official "values statement," Bethel aimed to live continually in God's dynamic life. Bethel was not content with a mere knowledge of God; instead, they sought to participate in *and experience* God's Trinitarian life. Bethel's desire for divine presence was not limited to the sacraments, spiritual disciplines, or official preaching of the church, but they looked to experience God *directly—* through the Holy Spirit. The unmediated union with the Spirit occurred socially through individual and corporate exchanges described as "spiritual encounters." For Bethel, Christ's presence in the Spirit was the wellspring of their vibrant spiritual life and the source of God's numinous power.

Weekend Worship Services

Bethel's attention to God's presence was most evident in their weekend worship services. Worship was a high priority at Bethel, considering the time, attention, and energy given to their gatherings. Bethel's worship services were loud, vibrant, and especially engaging for its participants. Most services comprised about six hundred to eight hundred people, but some could be as large as twelve hundred. As mentioned, Bethel hosted five weekend services, and with some services, long lines of people formed outside the sanctuary doors, waiting for worship to start. I visited all five Bethel weekend services, but my family and I usually attended the 9:15 a.m. service. The 9:15 a.m. service was their

---

1. Michael Gorman defines spirituality as "the lived experience of Christian belief." It is "the experience of God's love and grace in daily life" or "life in the Spirit" (*Cruciformity*, 2–3). Jürgen Moltmann defines spirituality as "life in God's Spirit, and a living relationship with God's Spirit" (*Spirit of Life*, 82).

20

smallest—about four hundred fifty people—held at a location off from their main campus.

When I first visited the 9:15 a.m. service, I was surprised by the presence of younger and older people in attendance. With both young and old present, I realized I had assumed Bethel was primarily a young person's church. During a typical service, a seven-person band led a packed room of worshipers who sang songs often on the theme of God's presence. The band was joined by female and male dancers on stage who waved flags and performed interpretative dances to the worship music. An artist accompanied the dance troupe on stage, painting interpretative art.

People responded verbally and physically during worship. Most people raised their hands while singing, while others danced in the aisle or gathered near the stage to get closer to the music, God, or both. It was common to see men, women, or children spinning, skipping, or waving flags. I once even witnessed a high-school male popping a "robot dance" during worship. The worship gathering was a sea of movement and raw emotion, suggesting a vibrant passion for God and strong enthusiasm within the church.

A typical Bethel worship service lasted about two hours, with about half of the time devoted to song and worship. Bethel pastors usually preached for about forty-five minutes. Some evening services could extend up to three to four hours long, depending on "how the Spirit was moving." During my four months of observation, I never sensed that the church curated its services to "attract" nonbelievers or grow church membership. Indeed, I could see how Bethel's highly expressive worship and enthusiasm could militate against some visitors returning. Pastor Bill Johnson often explained Bethel's approach, saying, "Our purpose is not to build a big church but big people." The worship of the congregation seemed thoroughly heartfelt and earnest. The energy in the room was neither forced nor contrived. Once the service ended, many members stayed in the room to converse with friends or receive prayer from ministers at the front. The desire for God's presence was palpable, reflected in the time, attention, and energy present at Bethel's worship services.

A POWERFUL PRESENCE

However, despite the energy and vitality present at Bethel Church, I heard how Bethel services were not to the tastes of everyone. For instance, I spoke with Erica, a wife and mother who had attended Bethel for eight months with her family. Erica and her family had commuted fifty minutes to Bethel but eventually left the church. When asked why they stopped attending, Erica replied, "It is too big and too difficult to find community." Erica and her family had since moved to Redding and coincidentally closer to Bethel, yet they still had decided *not* to return to the megachurch. They attend a noncharismatic church in town. Erica said she missed the practice of the supernatural gifts at her new church but enjoyed having the preaching of Scripture at the center of worship. Another person who did not enjoy Bethel's worship service was Emily, a family friend who used to attend the church I pastored in the Bay Area. While visiting my family and me in Redding over two weekends, Emily joined us for a Bethel service. However, Emily did not return a second time. When I asked why she did not want to attend another Bethel service, Emily, who rarely missed a weekend service at our previous church, said that she found the service too large and overstimulating.

Bill Johnson

Perhaps the person most responsible for Bethel's presence-centered spirituality was their senior leader, Bill Johnson. Johnson was Bethel's primary leader and speaker, but he liberally shared the pulpit with others. Johnson's onstage demeanor was even tempered, warm, and deliberate. He was not given to hyperbole or flash. He preached topically from Scripture, emphasizing themes such as God's kingdom, heaven-to-earth spirituality, and supernatural power. Johnson taught mainly from the Gospels and the Old Testament. Rarely did I hear him speak from the Epistles, except for an occasional proof text. Bill Johnson's presence-centered emphasis is also reflected in his writings. For example, in his book *Hosting the Presence*, Johnson calls participating in God's presence "the ultimate assignment." He writes, "It's important that we all find the 'one thing' that can become the reference point for the rest of the issues of life. And that one thing is the Presence of the Almighty God, resting upon us."[2]

Johnson's presence-centered message has significantly shaped his congregation. Other Bethel leaders and members often spoke about living from the place of God's presence. For example, the leader of Bethel's healing rooms once visited my BSSM revival group, a gathering of about sixty students. When I heard that the healing rooms director was visiting, I expected him to share testimonies of divine healing with our group. Instead, he led us in a two-hour contemplative prayer exercise focused on God's presence. This leader introduced the prayer exercise by saying it was an opportunity to "rest in God's presence." Indeed, I found the prayer exercise spiritually refreshing. While facilitating our group, the healing rooms director explained his approach to healing ministry. He said divine healing occurs not from the person praying but as "we extend the presence of Christ to the sick and hurting." Another instance when I heard a Bethel member refer to God's presence was during a Bethel outreach. The outreach consisted of praying for and counseling people visiting an abortion clinic in Redding (respectfully and from the sidewalk). As our team of five people gathered before the outreach to pray, I noticed the prayer of one team member, Hailey, a thirty-year-old wife and mother from Australia. Hailey opened our prayer time, saying, "Lord, I just want to serve you today from a place of your presence today." After the event, I noted Hailey's prayer and recorded it in my field notes.

Encounters and Power

"Encounter" was the word Bethel members often used to describe an intense experience of God's presence. Bethel viewed encounters as the primary means for members to grow in faith and character, similar to how Evangelicals see the role of Scripture. Encounters

2. Johnson, *Hosting the Presence*, 21.

involved direct and immediate experiences with God in Christ via his Spirit. Encounters were also evidential in nature, as people were visibly affected. In his book *Face to Face with God*, Bill Johnson writes, "[God] is to be known through encounters. . . . Many people are content to live with the concept of the presence of God in their lives, but they fail to enter the intended experience."[3] Encounters at Bethel could occur at any time, but they usually happened during intense occasions of corporate worship. An encounter could last minutes, hours, days, or weeks. A Bethel member's hope through an encounter was to experience God profoundly, leading to what they consider a "breakthrough" in one's personal and spiritual life. Bethel understood spiritual encounters akin to Moses's experience at the burning bush or Isaiah's heavenly vision, where a person's life was dramatically altered (Isa 6:1–6). Personal stories of profound encounters abounded at the church, often involving intense ecstatic experiences, dreams, visions, or God's mighty works.

Through divine encounters, Bethel members experienced God's presence and power. Therefore, Bethel members were encouraged to "seek encounters." In a sermon posted online, Johnson associates divine encounters with divine power, stating, "The real evidence of the baptism of the Holy Spirit is power. Many people are satisfied with good theology, and they stop short of the divine encounter." Johnson understands the purpose of Scripture as leading one toward a divine encounter. He continues, "The revelation of Scripture is to take us into an encounter with a Person that transforms us."[4]

Johnson understands the gospel of Christ in terms of God's power. In a social media post, he writes,

> The Gospel only comes in one form—one that transforms lives. We cannot separate the Gospel from the power of God, and when the moments of demonstration and victory come, we give those moments to God readily. But what about the moments of pain or loss, or when

3. Johnson, *Face to Face*, 22.

4. Johnson, "Receiving and Walking," 0:00–0:17.

BETHEL CHURCH: MAIN OBSERVATIONS

it didn't go the way we believed that it would? God is asking us to give Him those moments, too.[5]

At Bethel, a supernatural lifestyle of power was considered "normal" to the Christian life. Bethel takes seriously Jesus's words "Nothing is impossible with God" (Luke 1:37). In his book *When Heaven Invades Earth*, Johnson asserts, "It is abnormal for a Christian not to have an appetite for the impossible. . . . It has been written into our spiritual DNA to hunger for the impossibilities around us to bow at the name of Jesus."[6] Johnson and other Bethel leaders believed it was their mandate to do the "greater works" that Jesus commanded (John 14:12). By "greater works," Johnson and others understood Jesus's words as greater in *magnitude*, not just in number. Bethel was not content with anything less than power Christianity. In his book *Developing a Supernatural Lifestyle*, Kris Vallotton says, "We cannot be satisfied with illustrated sermons, great music, and friendly services. We have been called to see the power of darkness destroyed and our ruined cities restored."[7]

The presence of supernatural power at the church was one of the main reasons people moved to Redding to attend Bethel. For example, Scott was a thirty-two-year-old schoolteacher from a southern state who grew up in a Southern Baptist home. Scott moved to Redding to attend Bethel, explaining, "[Because] the power of God was here." Manuel was an Afro-Latino from Florida who had considered several ministry schools before choosing Bethel. Manuel only considered "supernatural" ministry schools because they "believe in God's miraculous power." Bethel's emphasis on God's supernatural power was reflected in their ministry school's name, Bethel School of *Supernatural* Ministry (BSSM). In a sermon at BSSM, Bill Johnson explained how other Christian leaders had initially scoffed at their inclusion of "supernatural" in the school's name. Johnson, however, said it was a defining moment for the church, adding, "And God has honored it." Even BSSM's official

5. Johnson, "Gospel only comes."

6. Johnson, *When Heaven Invades Earth*, 25.

7. Vallotton, *Developing a Supernatural Lifestyle*, 20.

25

mission statement focused on supernatural encounters: "We owe the world an encounter with Jesus."[8]

Encounters at Bethel were often accompanied by ecstatic physical manifestations, such as intense shaking, laughing, crying, or swoon-like falling. The enthusiastic expressions are concerning to many Evangelicals outside of Bethel.[9] However, for Bethel members, these powerful effects were evidence of God's presence. Bethel believed ecstatic experiences had biblical (and historical) support and were often essential to a person's growth with God. At Bethel, I witnessed individuals and groups manifesting ecstatically. Bethel leaders admitted that not every physical manifestation demonstrated at the church was "from God." However, they have chosen to extend relatively broad freedom to those manifesting ecstatically, out of respect for what God *may* be doing in a person's life.[10]

Bethel believed that God worked profoundly through physical manifestations. For example, Robyn was a thirty-something woman from Taiwan who grew up in a charismatic church. However, Robyn's church was not as ecstatically expressive as Bethel. Therefore she was skeptical and cautious when she first arrived. To Robyn, occasions of shaking, laughing, or falling just "seemed weird," she said. However, during corporate worship at BSSM, groups of students were manifesting physically with "holy laughter." As the laughter increased across the room, with other students joining in, Robyn's revival group pastor approached to pray for her. As the pastor prayed, he gently laid his hands on Robyn, and she soon shook uncontrollably. Robyn described the experience as "the power of God" coming upon her. In her words, Robyn suddenly fell to the floor, "overwhelmed by the presence of God." I asked Robyn if she had *willed herself* to the floor. She responded,

---

8. See https://bssm.net/culture/missions/, s.v. "Our Mission."

9. MacArthur, *Strange Fire*; Christina BRSLO, "False Prophesies."

10. Bethel imposed limits on manifestations only when they became too distracting to the general group experience. On two occasions, I witnessed a Bethel leader curtailing loud vocal manifestations because he felt they were disruptive to his preaching and the group's experience.

BETHEL CHURCH: MAIN OBSERVATIONS

"No, I fell; it just happened." Robyn described the experience as her "mind and body being separated." Robyn found herself laughing uncontrollably and "flipping like a fish [on the ground]." Robyn said she was conscious during the encounter, which lasted about thirty minutes. When asked about the fruit of the encounter, Robyn explained, "God removed irrational fears from my life." Robyn's irrational fears involved concerns over her physical safety while living in America. As a young, single female from Taiwan, Robyn had feared being physically attacked. Robyn said she had had no real reason for the fear, but she had struggled to even walk across the street or close her eyes during worship. However, during the encounter, Robyn felt an overwhelming sense of God's presence, power, and love. The result was that her fears disappeared. Even one year after the encounter, in a follow-up interview, Robyn said her irrational fears had not returned. The spiritual experience had a profound effect on Robyn's life.

Extreme Encounters

While at Bethel, I heard several testimonies of extreme encounters that challenged modern conceptions. One of the more dramatic stories I heard was from Kevin, a thirty-something Bethel pastor. Kevin and I met during a dinner party my wife and I hosted in our home. Kevin shared his story of miraculous healing, and I followed up with him later for an interview. Kevin's story involved growing up in a Southern Baptist home in the southern United States. While in his mid-twenties, Kevin developed a chronic digestive condition that made his stomach feel as if it was constantly on fire. Kevin's condition worsened significantly after a physician's mistake during a routine office visit. The attending physician, an intern, mistakenly administered Kevin too much hydrochloric acid. As Kevin swallowed an excessive amount of hydrochloric acid, he immediately lost consciousness. Once he regained consciousness, Kevin's field of vision was limited to a single beam of light in the corner of his eye. Although his vision eventually returned, Kevin could no longer consistently hold down food. Kevin's stomach ached

A POWERFUL PRESENCE

constantly, his skin turned ashen, and he lost significant amounts of weight. As a result of his condition, Kevin had to be administered six to seven allergy injections *per day* to treat his symptoms. Kevin's desperate plight lasted an unbearable *five years*—without relief. During this intense pain and suffering, Kevin lost hope for healing. He said he did not consider his Southern Baptist church a place that could help with his physical condition.

However, one day Kevin met up with a childhood friend who had recently attended a "supernatural" ministry school. The friend led Kevin through several Bible passages specific to divine healing. The friend explained that it was not God's will for Kevin to suffer but to heal him. The friend attributed Kevin's sickness to "a spirit of infirmity." Therefore, the friend laid his hands on Kevin's stomach and commanded the spirit of infirmity to come out. Soon after the prayer, Kevin's stomach began to growl—loudly. The growling lasted thirty seconds without stopping. Kevin said anyone in the room could have heard it. Kevin described the physical movement in his body as "the presence of chaos being ripped out." This "presence of chaos" then moved up and down his body "as if following a map." The chaos ended as if drawing a line down Kevin's spine. For the next five hours, Kevin said (humorously), he flatulated. Kevin and his friend stayed awake that night until 5 a.m., singing praises to God from a stolen Baptist hymnal. When Kevin woke up the following day, he had an unusual feeling—he felt hungry again! Hopeful yet cautious, Kevin tried eating again. Miraculously, he ate without any adverse effects. At that moment, Kevin *knew* he had been healed.

The supernatural healing changed Kevin's life. The experience led him to move to Bethel to be a part of a supernatural church. Kevin's physical healing also gave him hope to overcome unwanted same-sex attraction he had experienced since childhood. Kevin reasoned that if God could heal him physically, "[then] God could heal me emotionally and sexually too." Kevin reported that his same-sex desires receded over several years and that today, he was happily married, and he and his wife have three children together.

Questioning Encounters?

Despite Kevin and Robyn's life-changing encounter experiences, however, I also spoke with others at Bethel who expressed concern about some of the physical manifestations at the church. For example, David, a third-year, twenty-year-old BSSM student from California, questioned the authenticity of some people's encounters. David worried some students were merely "going along with the crowd." He also wondered whether some BSSM students were more interested in an emotional experience than actual communion *with God.*

I shared David's concern one day when I participated in a prayer gathering at BSSM. During the prayer gathering, a third-year BSSM student informed the group that the scheduled staff member could not make it, so he was filling in. The third-year student opened his prayer time rather energetically, exuberantly declaring, "Okay! Today, we are going after encounters!" As the student leader made the announcement, many students in the room cheered loudly. The third-year student then led the prayer session in a boisterous and enthusiastic manner. He repeated the phrase, "The fire of God! The fire of God!" Many in the group followed suit, matching the leader's volume and energy. The entire experience seemed "forced" to me, leaving me curious as to the student leader's goal with the prayer meeting. I wondered if his purpose was to energize the crowd or commune God in prayer. I felt uncomfortable with the whole experience and wrote about it in my field notes afterward.

Gift-Empowered Ministry

A second observation from my participant observation and intensive interviews was that ministry at Bethel Church was empowered through spiritual gifts (*charismata*). Bethel did not emphasize involving members in ministry programs or small groups, although they offered such spaces (e.g., home groups, age-specific fellowships, service ministries, etc.). Bethel encouraged members to discover, practice, and use their spiritual gifts. Of these gifts, Bethel emphasized the "power gifts" of faith, healing, miracles, and the vocal gifts of prophecy. Bethel encouraged members to exercise these spiritual gifts with believers and nonbelievers alike as a channel of God's dynamic power.

The Gift of Healing

Bethel emphasized the "power gifts" of 1 Cor 12:9, identified as faith, healing, and miracles. Bethel viewed the power gifts as a way for members to "walk in signs, wonders, and miracles," a common phrase at the church. Concerning the power gifts, the gift of healing received the most attention. For example, when Bill Johnson or other leaders shared testimonies of God's dynamic power, they often involved stories of divine healing. Also, the healing rooms was a marque ministry at church, serving over eight thousand people annually, according to its website.[11] At the healing rooms, visitors signed up for (free) healing prayer administered by Bethel-trained counselors. Healing prayer was also offered at the end of each Bethel weekend service by prayer counselors assembled at the front. The importance of healing ministry was evidenced by the historical figures BSSM students studied, healing revivalists like John Alexander Dowie, Maria Woodworth-Etter, and Aimee Semple McPherson.[12] BSSM students practiced healing prayer during local outreaches and foreign mission trips.

Bethel's position on divine healing was that it is always "God's will" to heal, with only a few exceptions. To support their position, Bethel leaders cited passages such as Matt 19:26 ("with God all things are possible") or emphasized how in the Gospels Jesus healed everyone who asked (e.g., Matt 4:23; Mark 1:29–34). Bethel argued that just as God "desires all people to be saved and come to the knowledge of the truth" (1 Tim 2:4), God desires all to be healed, even though not all are saved or healed. In this vein,

11. See https://www.bethel.com/ministries/healing-rooms.

12. Liardon, *God's Generals.*

BETHEL CHURCH: MAIN OBSERVATIONS

Bethel leaders readily admitted that not everyone who receives healing prayer is healed. For example, during a training I attended on how to lead and activate others in supernatural ministry, the class instructor, a Bethel leader known for healing ministry, explained that only about 30 percent of the people he prays for actually experience healing. Nonetheless, this leader held Jesus as the model for divine healing, believing that 100 percent of people *ought* to be healed. In principle, Bethel leaders expected "in faith" healing to occur on all occasions, even if that faith is not realized. This leader, known for his healing ministry, explained that he would pray for and expect healing even for "someone who was ninety-five years old and near death." He stated, "If I don't expect God to heal her, then I'm saying that I want death to be her Savior, not Jesus." On several occasions, I heard Bethel leaders praying for their church to be a "perfect-health zone." Again, sickness and disease were viewed as against God's will; therefore, like Jesus, the church should expect healing.

Bethel explained that divine healing could occur instantaneously or progressively. They referred to Jesus having to pray for the blind man *twice* or the ten lepers being healed "as they went on their way" as biblical examples of progressive healing (Mark 8:24–25; Luke 17:11–19). Bethel also distinguished between healing and miracles. Healing, they said, involved divine action through the body's natural processes, if not enhanced or accelerated. Miracles involved God's action that superseded the body's natural course. Considering this distinction, Bethel also referred to certain divine occurrences as "healing miracles," where the body is healed incommensurably, like blind eyes seeing, deaf ears hearing, or limbs being restored. In other words, while some healings may involve a miracle, not all healings are "miraculous." At Bethel, I heard testimonies (but never witnessed personally) from members who witnessed blind eyes, deaf ears, and malformed limbs being restored.

Thankfully, Bethel leaders never attributed responsibility or "a lack of faith" to the person receiving (or administering) healing prayer when healing did not occur. When healing did not occur, it was often understood as a "divine mystery." For example,

31

during my four-month observation at Bethel, Bill Johnson's wife, Beni Johnson, passed away after a long battle with cancer. Mrs. Johnson was the co-pastor of Bethel and a much-beloved figure at the church. After many months of fervent prayer on behalf of the congregation and countless others worldwide, news of Mrs. Johnson's death greatly saddened the church. However, the loss of Mrs. Johnson did not shake Bethel's faith in divine healing. In the weekend's sermon following his wife's passing, Bill Johnson spoke personally and emotionally about his wife—her life, faith, and legacy. He also reaffirmed their commitment to divine healing. He explained that although Christians believe God for healing, sometimes healing does not occur. Johnson understood his wife's lack of healing as "a divine mystery." In declaring his faith despite the lack of healing for his wife, Johnson explained, "I work for him; he does not work for me."

The Gift of Prophecy

In addition to power gifts (i.e., faith, healing, and miracles), the "vocal gift" of prophecy was prominent at the church. Prophecy was especially active at BSSM, where students learned to prophesy, similar to how Evangelicals learn to evangelize. BSSM students practiced prophesying with one another and with strangers during outreaches. For example, during one revival group meeting, my fellow students and I practiced giving prophetic words to fellow classmates we did not know well. We then provided feedback on the correspondence of those prophetic words. On another occasion, we wrote prophetic messages to people attending one of Bethel's annual conferences. Practicing prophecy was so prevalent that BSSM students joked, "You even receive [prophetic] words in the bathroom." Art imitated life one day as I received a prophetic word from a fellow student in the men's room. The BSSM student, whom I did not know, approached me saying that I reminded him of the character Atticus Finch from the movie *To Kill a Mockingbird*. The next time I saw this student (interestingly again in the bathroom), he handed me a copy of the book, explaining, "I felt led to give it to you." I understood the student to mean that he was inspired *prophetically* to give me the book. I accepted the copy and began reading it a few days later (but never finished it).

Bethel taught its members to utilize spiritual gifts outside the church as an entrée for evangelism. For example, David, a twenty-year-old BSSM student mentioned earlier, arrived at a local grocery store as part of a Friday night evangelism ministry. While at the grocery store, he gave a prophetic word to another twenty-something who was also shopping. David's prophetic word "spoke" to the man and opened a door to share the message of Jesus with him. The young man received Christ in the frozen food section of the store. The experience brought David considerable joy, especially since it was the first time he had led a stranger to faith in Christ. Bethel students would also offer healing prayer to people they met on the street, hoping to open doors for evangelism.

The spiritual gifts that received little attention at Bethel were the other gifts of 1 Cor 12 and Rom 12:6–8. They were gifts of service, exhortation, giving, administration, mercy, interpretation of tongues, and helps. (The "leadership gifts" of Eph 4:11 receive considerable attention and will be covered in the section below.) Surprisingly, the gift of tongues was not strongly emphasized at the church, as Bethel leaders seemed to assume most students practiced the gift already. Further, the fruit of the Spirit, as named in Gal 5:22–23, received light attention at Bethel and BSSM. Although Bethel leaders did talk about the need for holiness and purity, I noticed reticence regarding the Spirit's fruit, which was a significant departure from my evangelical circles.

Immediacy Through Spiritual Gifts

The practice of spiritual gifts fostered a strong sense of divine immediacy at the church. This immediacy was especially felt with the "power gifts" of faith, healings, miracles, and the vocal gifts of prophecy and words of knowledge. When a person received a prophetic word, it felt as if God sent it directly. For example, on one occasion, a friend approached me during congregational worship. He whispered to me over loud music, "I have a [prophetic] word for you." I invited my friend to share his prophetic word, and surprisingly, it strongly resonated with me. The prophetic word corresponded to a meaningful life decision I had considered just that morning. My friend had no way of knowing the issue I was wrestling with, adding to the strong sense of divine immanence I felt. I shared with my friend how his words encouraged me and thanked him for sharing them. We both rejoiced in God's goodness of a timely word.

Like prophecy, healing ministry also conveyed a strong sense of God's immediacy. When people experienced divine healing, they felt God's personal care and touch. For example, my wife and I were visited by friends from England during my time of participant observation. The wife attended Bethel's healing rooms to receive prayer for tinnitus, which she had experienced since she was a teenager. Now in her forties, the tinnitus was so severe that she had difficulty hearing others on the telephone. Our friend had never received healing prayer before, and she admitted later she was skeptical when entering the healing rooms. However, her concerns were alleviated when her tinnitus was healed instantly after receiving prayer. Our friend was shocked and exceedingly grateful. In speaking with our friend a year later, the tinnitus had not returned. Our friend said that she felt especially loved and cared for by God due to the healing.

God's immediacy was enhanced by the practice of the laying on of hands, a common practice at the church. The custom of laying on of hands is well attested to in Scripture (Num 8:10; 27:18; Mark 7:32; 10:16; Luke 4:40; Acts 8:17; 1 Tim 4:14), and Bethel often practiced it during moments of corporate and intercessory prayer. The practice seemed to break down personal barriers and enhance immediacy between God and his people. As a protocol, Bethel taught members on appropriate (and inappropriate) ways to practice the laying of hands.

BETHEL CHURCH: MAIN OBSERVATIONS

Leadership Gifts

In addition to the power and vocal gifts of 1 Cor 12:9–11, Bethel emphasized the "leadership gifts" of Eph 4:11. In his Letter to the Ephesians, Paul writes, "And [God] gave the apostles, the prophets, the evangelists, the pastors and teachers, to equip the saints for the work of ministry, for the building up of the body of Christ." In this passage, the gifts are not specific services but leaders (i.e., "the apostles, the prophets, the evangelists," etc.). Many Evangelicals balk at the contemporary designation of apostles and prophets, but Bethel considered these roles essential to the church and its mission. For example, Bill Johnson was considered Bethel's apostle, although he never referred to himself as such. Kris Vallotton was referred to as the church's in-house prophet. Vallotton clarified that his "prophetic authority" did not extend to other churches but to Bethel alone. In a sermon to BSSM students, Kris Vallotton described the role of apostles as those who "change culture." Bethel viewed modern apostles as different from the Twelve who walked with Jesus. Bethel leaders argued that the twelve apostles served a unique role as founders of the church, whereas modern-day apostles are sent out to start new works of God.[13] A prophet's role was to bring forth an inspired and timely word to the church for their "upbuilding and encouragement and consolation" (1 Cor 14:3). Prophetic utterances involved both forthtelling and foretelling (1 Cor 14:24–25; Acts 21:10–12). Bethel never attributed prophetic declarations with equal weight and authority to Scripture but considered them "inspired speech." Bethel encouraged all prophetic words to be tested and weighed against Scripture (1 Cor 14:29; 1 Thess 5:20–21). Because prophetic utterances were considered Spirit-inspired, Bethel affirmed the belief in modern-day revelation. Bethel understood Scripture as "special revelation" but prophetic declarations as "directional" or "inspirational" revelation. Considering the relationship between Scripture and inspired speech like prophecy, Bethel described the canon of Scripture as "the floor" of revelation rather than

13. Bethel, *Rediscover Bethel*, episode 4, "Church, Ministry."

its "ceiling." As the metaphorical "floor" of revelation, Scripture serves as the church's foundation upon which other inspired revelations are considered but never attributed with equal authority. Bethel contended that God builds upon but never contradicts his special revelation in Scripture. As such, Bethel leaders considered it essential for the church to be led by Spirit *and* truth (John 4:24). Bethel asserted that all believers could and should utter prophetic words, but only those especially anointed are considered "prophets."

Bethel prioritized the ministries of apostles and prophets, drawing from passages like 1 Cor 12:28. Here Paul writes, "And God has appointed in the church first apostles, second prophets, third teachers, then miracles, then gifts of healings, helping, administrating, and various kinds of tongues." Bethel did not see a hierarchy of church leadership but a *prioritizing and sequential ordering* of leadership (viz, *first* apostles, *second* prophets, *third* teachers, *then* miracles, etc.). Bethel held that when apostles and prophets are in place *first* (not "in first place"), then other ministries, such as pastors and teachers, can flourish. At Bethel, leaders with apostolic and prophetic gifts were known for their bold faith and supernatural ministry. Pastors and teachers were valued for their stabilizing force and personal care. Bethel did not emphasize the role of evangelists as witnessed in evangelical circles, although some leaders within the community were considered "evangelists."

Bethel held that the roles of apostles and prophets were essential to Christianity's future. In a sermon at BSSM, Vallotton attributed much of Bethel's growth and influence to their prioritizing apostles and prophets. Vallotton shared a "vision" he had received in a dream one night when asleep. In the dream, Vallotton said the Lord spoke to him, saying, "In the future, apostolic fathers will replace denominationalism." He distinguished apostleship from denominationalism as the former was based on familial relationships, whereas the latter was "based on [theological] agreement." Vallotton viewed apostolic fathers as forging stronger bonds than denominations. He argued that apostles allow for theological disagreement, whereas denominations do not. Vallotton was quick to distinguish between denominations and denominational-*ism*. He stated that denominationalism (not denominations) hindered the gospel's advancement. During my observational period, Bethel never officially identified itself with the New Apostolic Reformation,[14] at least as some critics have defined it.[15] However, it was clear that Bethel affirmed the practice of modern apostles and prophets.

Women in Leadership

One crucial feature of Bethel was women in prominent leadership positions at the church. For example, Beni Johnson was Bethel's co-pastor until her passing. Women preached at weekend services, annual conferences, BSSM events, and weekend retreats. Women were considered "apostles," "prophets," and "pastors," and other leadership designations. Several BSSM leaders and revival group pastors were women. Women were the lead pastors of two Bethel church plants in other cities. Bethel defended its position on women in leadership from passages such as Acts 2:17, arguing that since the Holy Spirit was poured out on "all flesh," women were permitted to preach, teach, and lead like men. In Acts 2, Peter explains, "[Both] your sons and daughters will prophesy . . . your male servants and female servants" (vv. 17–18). Bethel also referenced "Junia" from Paul's Letter to the Romans as a possible woman apostle (16:7). Prominent women from revival history were held up as examples to follow, such as Maria Woodworth-Etter, Aimee Semple McPherson, and Kathryn Kuhlman.[16]

"Shiny People"

However, despite the overwhelming positive influence of the spiritual gifts at Bethel, I heard a common critique of the church. The

14. Wagner, *Churchquake.*

15. Pivec and Geivett, *Counterfeit Kingdom,* 215–18.

16. Liardon, *God's Generals.*

critique concerned the disproportionate attention given to those members who operated in the more spectacular gifts, such as healing, miracles, and inspired utterances, than to those who did not. I heard from several Bethel members that those who operated in the "less sensational" gifts, such as service, administration, helps, received less attention from leadership. This lesser attention even extended to those who operated in the pastoring and teaching gifts, at least when compared to apostles and prophets. The concern of disproportionate attention (or "favor" as it was called) was especially prominent at BSSM, which focused on developing future revivalists. At BSSM, students were keenly aware of which students "found favor" with BSSM leadership and those who did not. The students who "found favor" usually operated in the power gifts and often manifested ecstatically. For example, John, a twenty-something BSSM student, shared how he felt those who operated in the power gifts received more praise and attention from Bethel leadership. Those who received increased attention were referred to by John and others, pejoratively, as "shiny people." They were considered "shiny" because their supernatural gifting seemed to "shine" or "glisten" more to the BSSM leadership. Perhaps the emergence of "shiny people" resulted from BSSM serving as a school, not simply a church, where achievement is praised. Nonetheless, the presence of "shiny people" was a common concern in my interviews and conversations.

Revival as Imagination and Ethos

In addition to Bethel's presence-based spirituality and gift-centered ministry, the theme of revival wedded together Bethel's life and imagination. The church's supernatural faith was heightened by anticipating God's next great outpouring of the Spirit. The hope for revival significantly shaped every aspect of the church. From official church statements to historical figures BSSM students studied, revival served as Bethel's vision and values. For example, the church's official mission statement was a revival statement: "Bethel's mission is revival—the personal, regional, and global expansion of God's kingdom through his manifest presence."[17] BSSM students gathered not in "small groups" but "revival groups." Leaders in charge of these groups were called "revival group pastors." BSSM's mission was to raise up a generation of "future revivalists." Revivalists were defined as: "A believer who is focused and passionate, willing to pay any price to live in community, purity, and power, because they are loved by God, whose manifest presence transforms lives and culture."[18]

BSSM students studied past revivals and the revivalists who led them. Figures such as John Wesley, Charles Finney, William Seymour, Aimee Semple McPherson, Kathryn Kuhlman, and Oral Roberts were heroes to follow.[19] Even D. L. Moody, an evangelical stalwart, garnered attention and praise (perhaps due to his belief in the "second blessing of the Holy Spirit"). However, Billy Graham, whom Bill Johnson was named after, did not receive much attention (perhaps due to his not recognizing a second blessing of the Spirit). Older Bethel members shared stories of past revivals in which they participated, like the Jesus People movement, Brownsville, or the Toronto outpouring. BSSM students were offered classes like "Revival Apologetics," providing a biblical and historical defense of the ecstatic manifestations often accompanying revivals. Bethel's primary aspirations were not evangelism, spiritual formation, discipleship, social justice, or Christ's return. Instead, Bethel hoped for God's next great spiritual outpouring, believing that evangelism, discipleship, and mission would follow when God's people are set ablaze with holy fire.

Bill Johnson said his personal life and ministry were reared for revival. The influence of John Wimber's supernatural ministry and Toronto's Father's Blessing were mentioned previously. When Johnson first arrived at Bethel as its senior pastor, he informed the congregation, "I was born for revival." Johnson recounted how he cried out day and night to God, praying for revival. He said, "God,

17. See https://www.bethel.com/about.

18. Farrelly, "Revivalist Lifestyle."

19. Johnson, *Defining Moments*.

I want more of You at any cost! I will pay any price!"[20] In *Face to Face with God*, Johnson recounts the dramatic nighttime encounter that set his course for revival. He writes,

> I went from being in a dead sleep to being wide-awake in a moment. Unexplainable power began to pulsate through my body. It was as if I had been plugged into a wall socket with a thousand volts of electricity flowing through my body. An extremely powerful being seemed to have entered the room, and I could not function in His presence. My arms and legs shot out in silent explosions as this power was released through my hands and feet. The more I tried to stop it, the worse it got. I soon discovered that this was not a wrestling match I was going to win. I heard no voice, nor did I have any visions. This was the most overwhelming experience of my life. It was raw power. It was God. He had come in response to the prayer I had been praying.[21]

As a result of the experience, Johnson said he had been committed to revival ever since. In a sermon at BSSM, Johnson revealed his heart's cry: "I was willing to look like a fool to the city I love if it meant experiencing 'the more of God.'" He promised God never to take his hands off the wheel of revival if God were to send it.

Revival Fire

The image most often associated with revival at the church was fire. Fire was a dominant theme among Bethel's songs, logos, sermons, and prayers. BSSM students and leaders often spoke of "keeping the flame of one's heart burning for the Lord." A believer known for her or his passion for God was considered spiritually "on fire." Enthusiastic BSSM students were invited to the "Burn Class" for further training in revival culture. Biblical narratives like Moses's encounter at the burning bush or Solomon's Temple's eternal flame painted vivid pictures of the Spirit's light, heat,

20. Johnson, *Face to Face*, 7.
21. Johnson, *Face to Face*, 7.

BETHEL CHURCH: MAIN OBSERVATIONS

and intensity. Bethel understood itself like OT priests tending to God's fire at the temple.

The sensational events of Pentecost (Acts 2) served as Bethel's paradigm for revival.[22] No other biblical story shaped Bethel's imagination and ethos more than Pentecost. At Pentecost, the heavens opened, tongues of fire descended, and the people of God manifested ecstatically. The miraculous events of Pentecost caused wonder as well as ridicule. Now filled with the Holy Spirit, Peter, who fifty days earlier had denied Christ, preached boldly about his resurrection and the promised Holy Spirit. As a result of Peter's message, three thousand people were saved, and the church of Christ was born. The spectacular scene of Pentecost—the heavens parting, fire descending, enthusiastic utterances, and bold preaching—shaped Bethel's revival expectations. Unusual or ecstatic manifestations were welcomed at the church—even encouraged, for they were signs of the Spirit's activity. Bethel talked openly about "not being offended" by God's unusual ways. Bethel members were aware of and even playfully joked about the ridicule and skepticism they faced from others regarding their unusual enthusiasm. Bethel did not seek to "restore an Acts 2 church" but sought the next great outpouring of the Spirit.

Ecstatic Experiences

Exposure to Bethel's revival culture helped me better understand the initially confusing aspects of the church. In particular, the shaking, falling, and excessive laughing or crying were manifestations I had limited exposure to before coming to Bethel. These ecstatic expressions were a significant cause of concern to some local Redding Evangelicals I interviewed. One Redding senior pastor criticized Bethel for permitting and encouraging the manifestations. He argued that leaders of past revivals discouraged people from manifesting ecstatically.

---

22. Only Ezekiel's vision of the valley of dry bones was second to Bethel's understanding of revival (Ezek 36–37).

One of the first ecstatic expressions I witnessed at Bethel was during a BSSM class I attended. (As a point of reference, BSSM was typically more ecstatically expressive than Bethel's general congregation.) On this occasion, a BSSM revival group pastor was scheduled to lead the class, but her third-year student announced that the pastor might be late to arrive. The reason given by the third-year student for the pastor's possible lateness surprised me. He said, "She's encountering the Lord right now, so I don't know when she will be here." By "encountering the Lord," I understood the intern to mean that the pastor was "drunk in the Spirit," a common phenomenon at BSSM. However, the issue was quickly resolved when the pastor arrived shortly after the announcement. After apologizing for being a few minutes late, the pastor confessed as she collected herself, "You'll have to bear with me. I'm still a little drunk [in the Spirit]." The pastor then began to teach the class. As a teaching pastor myself, I could not imagine entering a teaching occasion being what they considered "spiritually drunk." I wondered how her spiritually inebriated state would affect her teaching. However, to my great surprise, the pastor was exceptional. She brought an African American preaching style (herself being African American) involving "call-and-response" and powerful testimonies of God's action. I was deeply moved by her message. I recorded the event in my field notes after the class.

As mentioned, I did not understand these and other expressions initially, that is, until I spoke with Becky, a longtime Bethel member. Interviewing Becky was recommended to me by two Bethel pastors who described her as the official/unofficial historian of the church. Becky was a middle-aged woman and a published author. She had also served as a missionary to the Middle East for a period. Becky was present before and after Bill Johnson's arrival at Bethel; therefore, I reasoned that her extensive knowledge and experience at Bethel would help me understand the church.

As Becky and I sat down together at a local coffee shop, she opened by saying, "When the revival started at Bethel . . ." She then proceeded to recount some of the historical moments of the church, such as Bill Johnson's arrival and a visit by revivalist

Randy Clark. After hearing about some of these significant moments, which was helpful, I returned to her earlier words. I asked her what she meant when she said, "When the revival started at Bethel . . ." It was the first time I had heard of a revival occurring *at Bethel*. Becky shared how a great outpouring of the Spirit broke out soon after Bill Johnson's arrival. The spiritual awakening was so significant that "people were laying all over the floor." In saying, "people were laying all over the floor," I understood Becky to mean that many Bethel members were manifesting ecstatically in various ways (e.g., falling, swooning, laughing, and crying). Bethel leadership was so excited about the outpouring that they canceled all services and staff meetings to further attend to the Lord in prayer and worship. As Becky continued to share this story of revival, I noticed she never mentioned how the revival ended. Indeed, I noticed that Becky talked as if the revival *was still occurring*. Realizing this, I asked Becky, "Wait, do some people at Bethel believe that the church is still in a revival?" Becky did not disagree but smiled wryly and said, "The revival *has matured*." She explained that the revival had matured by producing ministries such as Bethel Music, the healing rooms, BSSM, and the many other ministries at the church.

Becky's response revealed something important about Bethel's imagination and ethos. Becky's response showed that she and many others at Bethel—including Bethel leadership—believed that the church had experienced revival in the 1990s and that *this revival was continuing*. This insight helped me understand Bethel's revival culture and why they permitted—even encouraged—leaders to become "spiritually drunk." For Bethel, these ecstatic expressions were *manifestations of the Spirit* and evidence of God's supernatural power. Revival was what Bill Johnson was born for. Bill Johnson and other Bethel leaders had hoped for a continuous, nonstop revival. Therefore, Bethel leaders encouraged ecstatic manifestations, believing God was powerfully at work within them.

Summary

Three main observations emerged during my immersion and intensive interviews at Bethel Church. The observations were that Bethel Church (1) practiced a presence-centered spirituality, (2) facilitated ministry through spiritual gifts, and (3) viewed revival as its imagination and ethic. All three factors supported and enhanced the church's belief and practice of God's supernatural power. For example, Bethel's presence-centered spirituality provided a *theological* basis for God's active power. God's presence was the source and sphere of his numinous power. Bethel's emphasis on the spiritual gifts provided the *ecclesial* foundation for exercising divine power at the church. God's dynamic power was evident as church members served through spiritual gifts—especially the "power gifts" (i.e., faith, healings, and miracles) and the vocal gift of prophecy. Bethel's hope and imagination for revival served as its *missiological* goal. Bethel viewed the Pentecostal Spirit as one who empowers the church to extend God's kingdom into the world. Bethel believed the gospel would reach the nations when the church was reignited with new life and fire. These three foci of presence-based spirituality, spiritual gifts, and revival consisted of Bethel's version of legitimate New Testament Christianity.

Chapter 3

Faith in Modernity: Our Cultural-Theological Condition

[Western culture] is the most powerful, most pervasive and (with the possible exception of Islam) the most resistant to the gospel of all the cultures which compete for power in our global city.—Lesslie Newbigin, *A Word in Season*

BETHEL CHURCH'S UNDERSTANDING AND practice of supernatural power did not occur in a vacuum. Bethel exercised its faith in a cultural context amid its relations with the world. As chapter 1 states, *culture* is a people's historical, religious, political, geographical, and relational world.[1] And the culture that Bethel finds itself in is the twenty-first-century modern West. Modern culture has developed over centuries and profoundly impacts how Bethel and other churches practice faith today. Modern culture directly and indirectly shapes the church's identity and sense of responsibility. Take, for example, Bethel's use of the word "supernatural" in its ministry school's name. Bethel School of *Supernatural* Ministry indicates how Bethel understands its relations with God, ministry practice, and involvement in the world. Bethel's

---

1. Brown, *Scripture as Communication*, 191.

inclusion of "supernatural" reflects the church's posture within a modern frame. A look at how Bethel practices its faith within the modern Western landscape will illuminate how God is at work there. In this chapter, I draw upon Charles Taylor's idea of the immanent frame to better understand Bethel's practice of supernatural faith in modern culture.

Faith in the Modern Age: The Immanent Frame

Charles Taylor is a professor emeritus of philosophy at McGill University and a professing Catholic. He has written extensively on political philosophy, the philosophy of social science, and the history of philosophy. In *A Secular Age*, Taylor provides an extensive account of how the conditions of faith changed in the West during the modern period. Taylor describes how belief in God shifted—from being taken for granted to being highly suspicious. Taylor asks, "[Why] was it virtually impossible not to believe in God, in say, 1500 in our Western society, while in 2000 many of us find this not only easy, but even inescapable?"[2] Taylor explores *how* faith changed in the West—not *when* or *what* occurred in this tidal shift. He asks how the West moved from a period during Christendom of assuming God's existence to today when many are skeptical of God. What social developments made belief in God difficult, whereas previously, it was woven into every area of life? Taylor presents the idea of "the immanent frame" to describe today's existential landscape.

Taylor argues that the immanent frame is how modern people inhabit a secular age. The immanent frame operates like a cultural "map" where life is navigated through a natural rather than a supernatural order.[3] The immanent frame is a modern social construction (i.e., frame) where the world is understood primarily as immanent or natural. One author describes the immanent frame as a "cultural shortcut" that shapes us by interpreting most

2. C. Taylor, *Secular Age*, 25.

3. I received this insight from Andrew Root, *Churches and the Crisis*, 12.

FAITH IN MODERNITY: OUR CULTURAL-THEOLOGICAL CONDITION

of "our relations as immanent contingencies, rather than next to or inside transcendent relations."[4] The immanent frame sees the world as a mechanistic universe of causal laws where meaning is derived without reference to God or the transcendent. Taylor says the immanent frame operates at a subconscious level, not as a worldview or social theory, but as a "social imaginary."[5] As a social imaginary, the frame shapes "the way ordinary people 'image' their social surroundings, and this is often not expressed in theoretical terms; it is carried in images, stories, legends, etc."[6] The immanent frame pushes divine mystery and action away from the center of the Western imagination.[7] Taylor does not seek to "get behind," ignore, or demolish the immanent frame. He wants to understand how people of faith live inside it.

North American churches like Bethel knowingly or unknowingly inhabit the immanent frame as participants in Western culture. The immanent frame is a part of our shared cultural experience. However, various churches will hold different "takes" on the immanent frame considering their cultural-theological positions. These cultural "takes" shape and reflect how they understand God's action in the world.

From Enchantment to Disenchantment

According to Taylor, the immanent frame changes how people perceive and experience reality. The author says the world shifted during modernity—from a place of enchantment to disenchantment. During premodern times, the world was alive and enchanted with spirits, demons, and moral forces. Physical objects and space were "charged" with meaning and held supranatural power. In medieval times, people believed such forces could influence and even possess them. Taylor observes that the line between

4. Root, *Churches and the Crisis*, 12.
5. C. Taylor, *Secular Age*, 171–72.
6. C. Taylor, *Secular Age*, 172.
7. Root, *Churches and the Crisis*, 206.

personal agency and impersonal force was not sharply drawn in premodern times.[8] Accordingly, these "charged" objects and spirits could affect people and things, influencing sicknesses, cures, diseases, ships on the sea, hail, lightning, and storms.

However, as the West moved from a premodern to a modern age, enchantment gave way to disenchantment, and the world became a mechanical, causal universe. As disenchantment grew, reality shifted from transcendence to immanence. In other words, the world turned from a created kingdom into an impersonal cosmos of causal laws. A created kingdom runs by a network of personal relationships, but an impersonal cosmos is ruled by the pushes and pulls of mechanical forces. The world as an impersonal cosmos reduces reality into sheer immanence, presenting a natural universe that is self-enclosed and self-sufficient. Taylor says transcendence was still possible in the modern age, but it was much harder to come by. The author describes any aspect of contemporary culture that "tips" the immanent frame toward a closed construal a "closed world structure."[9] Closed world structures have ways of restricting our grasp of transcendent reality. Furthermore, closed world structures go "a long way to explaining the unjustified force of the mainstream account of secularization, as well as the disinterest in and contempt for religion which frequently accompanies it."[10]

Taylor contends that God was displaced from the Western imagination during this modern period as the human person became central. In this way, reality became exclusively *subjective* and *humanistic*. Human agents and potentialities determined meaning—not God or objects of nature. Also, meaning was now apprehended through an individual's reason rather than divine revelation. Human beings became "enlightened" through reason alone. Kant's "dare to know" was modernity's call to courage, as everyone was now a skeptic. Indeed, in modernity, the skeptic is perceived as more intelligent and courageous than the "believer." Yet, people still felt "haunted" by transcendence. Human beings

8. C. Taylor, *Secular Age*, 32.

9. C. Taylor, *Secular Age*, 551–92.

10. C. Taylor, *Secular Age*, 551.

FAITH IN MODERNITY: OUR CULTURAL-THEOLOGICAL CONDITION

felt whispers of the divine, as they longed for mystery inside the enclosure. Materialism, hyper-spirituality, the occult, and psychedelics are some of the ways modern people sought mystery inside the enclosure.

New Understanding of the Self

As the world of disenchantment emerged, so did a new understanding of the self. Modernity yielded a "very different existential condition," says Taylor.[11] The author describes the self during premodern times as *porous*. The porous self was open to transcendence and susceptible to outside forces. The line between the self and the world of spirits, demons, and forces was "thin." However, a new "buffered" self emerged during modernity as the cosmos enclosed. The buffered self lives steeped in immanence and insulated from transcendence. The human self was no longer vulnerable to outside forces such as spirits and demonic forces but drew meaning from its own autonomous order.[12] Moreover, the shift from a porous to buffered self did not axiomatically replace belief in God. Taylor says the buffered self still needed a "safe place" to retreat. That safe place became the rational mind. The rational mind was considered the "neutral" safe haven for the self to "objectively" grasp the reality of a mechanical universe. Taylor describes the modern human mind as "bounded." Through the subjective rational mind, the self is bounded from external influences as the focus now becomes the *interior* world of the human person. In this way, modernity made atheism think*able*, at least according to the individualistic, self-determined, self-expressive self.

Taylor describes the contemporary life of the buffered self as experiencing "cross-pressures." He says, "The whole culture experiences cross-pressures, between the draw of the narratives of closed immanence on one side, and the sense of their inadequacy on the other, strengthened by encounter with existing

11. C. Taylor, *Secular Age*, 41.
12. C. Taylor, *Secular Age*, 38–39.

milieux of religious practice, or just by some imitations of the transcendent."[13] The buffered self experiences cross-pressures when caught between various earthly and ethereal options. On the one hand, modern people consider it their responsibility to construct the meaning on their own, but on the other hand, people are overwhelmed by the vapidity of modern life.

Churches and the Crisis of Decline

Andrew Root is a scholar who has explored Charles Taylor's insights on the immanent frame and has mined them for the church.[14] In *Churches and the Crisis of Decline*, Root considers Taylor's insights regarding the immanent frame with what Root calls the church's current "crisis of decline." Root holds that many North American churches and church leaders today feel anxious because of declining membership and waning social influence. The decrease in church membership and drop in social influence has pushed the church toward the edges of the Western imagination, causing churches and church leaders to feel displaced, which feels like a crisis.

Strategies to Address Decline

Root observes that church leaders employ various strategies to address the apparent church crisis of decline. He says churches that see the crisis *as decreased church membership* often look to resources to reverse the decline. These churches seek to leverage human and material capital toward growing church membership. The cry from these churches is "More!" "If we only had more money and manpower, then we could fulfill our mission," they say. Root finds the strategy of accumulating resources most common among conservative churches. In this score, the megachurch is

13. C. Taylor, *Secular Age*, 595.

14. See Root: *Faith Formation in Secular Age*; *Pastor in Secular Age*; *Congregation in Secular Age*.

FAITH IN MODERNITY: OUR CULTURAL-THEOLOGICAL CONDITION

seen as the evangelical success story. With its apparent abundance of human and material capital, the megachurch is viewed as a victor over the growing secularism and best positioned to fulfill the church's mission of evangelism. Churches that see resources as the solution to decline often rely on the "entrepreneur pastor" for leadership. The promise of the entrepreneur pastor is that he or she can successfully acquire more human and material resources for the church's mission. Also, modern business management principles are adopted to make the congregation run more "efficiently." Root says that leaders of these churches often operate their churches like modern-day corporations, utilizing the latest modern management techniques to grow membership. He writes,

> As the church started to feel losses toward the end of the twentieth century, all of the answers to beat decline were borrowed from hypercapitalism. For example, congregational life turned not to prayer, confession, sacramental ontologies, and discernment of the Spirit as much as to direct marketing, business structuring, customer focus groups, efficacy budgets, and spaces that feel like malls.[15]

In addition to churches that see the crisis of decline as a loss of church membership, Root describes other churches that view the crisis as *a loss of social relevance*. Churches that see the crisis as a loss of relevance were most common among liberal churches says the author.[16] In this score, progressive churches look to reposition themselves as socially and politically relevant in modern society. Social justice initiatives are at the forefront of these churches' concerns and efforts. These churches hope to lead on the pressing social issues of the day, thereby making the church relevant again. Leadership at these churches often takes the form of "the activist pastor." The activist pastor artfully identifies the relevant social injustices and successfully marshals the church's membership toward them. Root says that these justice initiatives sometimes take the form of identity politics. Bethel Church and the other Redding churches with whom I spoke did not express

15. Root, *Churches and the Crisis*, 18.

16. For example, see Yancey, "Who's More Political?"

liberal or progressive sentiments; therefore, the strategy of social relevance was not prominent among them.

What Gives Life?

In exploring the various strategies churches adopt to address the apparent crisis of decline, Root asks a crucial question: *What gives life?*[17] Root wants to know what gives Christian churches life and vitality. The author sees the church's strategies of accumulating resources or relevance essentially as a quest for life.[18] Church leaders employ these strategies, hoping to produce life for their congregations. However, Root sees the strategies of resources and relevance as accommodations to the immanent frame. Churches that trust in the accumulation of resources or relevance accept the reductions of modernity because these strategies implicitly restrict the view of God's actions in the world. These strategies "tip" ministry toward a "closed world structure." A congregation's hope in resources or relevance reflects a limited understanding of God's action inside the immanent frame. Instead of producing life, therefore, these strategies obscure God's presence and power in the world.

Root observes that by adopting the strategies of resources or relevance, the *expenditure of human energy* becomes paramount. The expenditure of human energy becomes paramount when church leaders trust in the accumulation of resources or relevance for *spiritual life*. Even though churches may adopt the strategies of resources or relevance in the hope of producing life, in the end, they are accommodations to the immanent frame since they restrict rather than open space for God's action.

17. Root, *Churches and the Crisis*, 13–16.

18. Dallas Willard understands life in terms of power. He writes, "What is life? In all its various levels and types, life is *power to act and respond in specific kinds of relations*" (*Hearing God*, 148; emphasis in original).

FAITH IN MODERNITY: OUR CULTURAL-THEOLOGICAL CONDITION

Being-Mode vs. Having-Mode

Another problem for congregations that trust in the expenditure of energy (either for resources or relevance) is they shift from "being-mode" to "having-mode." Being-mode and having-mode reflect two different approaches to life that modern people confuse. Being-mode involves being present in *mutual* relationships. Being-mode emphasizes mutual relationships and being present with and for one another. Being-mode represents something that we inhabit rather than possess. As Root states repeatedly, we cannot *have* a relationship; we can only *be* in a relationship. Being-mode for churches involves *being present with* God, each other, and the world. Being-mode is a response to being encountered by God in Christ, who is accessible through his Spirit. Having-mode is different than being-mode. Churches in having-mode seek "life" through possessing someone or something. Having-mode could involve possessing more members, resources, or relevance. Churches in having-mode seek to possess God and have his resources rather than abiding in his presence. Having-mode is an attitude consistent with modernity since it seeks life through control, certainty, or domination. Churches in having-mode believe they can control outcomes through methods, procedures, or programs. Root observes that when activity takes no account of being and seeks only having, there is "no distinction between activity and busyness."[19] Having-mode obscures God's action in the world by making the church the center of its story. Further, churches in having-mode eventually become dehumanizing and alienating. Root observes,

> Like modern factories, churches built for modern religion alienate people by accelerating their actions, making even their religious activities about the expenditure of energy. Unable to recognize the event of the living God's encounter in a living world, instead of asking its people to seek a God who is God, the church anxiously

19. Root, *Churches and the Crisis*, 127.

asks them to expend energy in activities that will keep the congregation afloat.[20]

Resonance Is Life

In exploring the question *What gives life?*, Root draws upon the modern concept of resonance.[21] Root believes resonance holds promise for understanding God's action inside the immanent frame. Root does not believe the church can escape the reductions of the age until it relinquishes a modern form of action, viewed mostly as energy expenditure. He writes,

> [It's] my contention that the church will be unable, even with its best desires and efforts, to escape the reductions (and hidden false norms) of late modernity and its immanent frame until it reconceives its own action, and does so theologically.[22]

The author contends that resonance enables the church to reimagine its own action. Resonance is the idea of "being in relationship with—connected to—something outside of yourself."[23] By emphasizing relationships, resonance provides a hopeful *alternative form of action* in the modern age. Resonance confronts and critiques modernity's dominant form of action since "resonance as a form of action upholds, and necessitates otherness."[24] Otherness—encountering other persons in free, mutual relations—is essential to resonance. Resonance is a way of *being* with others, over against *having them*. Resonance also produces *life*. Life is produced when people encounter God, each other, and creation in mutually free, loving, and holy relations. The church finds life in the modern age through resonance rather than the expenditure of energy.

---

20. Root, *Churches and the Crisis*, 130–31.
21. Rosa, *Resonance*.
22. Root, *Churches and the Crisis*, 166.
23. Root, *Churches and the Crisis*, 167.
24. Root, *Churches and the Crisis*, 167.

In any age, the church finds life through its union with Christ. Resonance occurs when the church encounters the resurrected One in the space of its gathering. When the church encounters Christ, it encounters its *Savior* and *Lord*. As such, resonance involves dialogue. A dialectic occurs between Christ and his church as they mutually encounter each other in free and loving relations (2 Cor 13:14; Phil 2:1). The dialectic between Christ and his church creates an opening within the immanent frame, rather than being restricted by it. As Root observes, "Because there is truly otherness, which can only be known through the other's own free action, the immanent frame remains open."[25] Resonance allows the church to participate in God's free action through life-giving relationships. This dialectic occurs between the material and spiritual, temporal and eternal, and earthly and heavenly. Root says the Christian faith loses life when it loses its dialectic. He writes, "Life is birthed inside the tension in the dialectic."[26]

Resonance is more than emotive expressivism. Resonance involves emotion, but it is not reduced to mere emotion. If emotions were the goal of resonance, then resonance would become a self-enclosed act, leading to emotional-*ism*. Emotionalism is a form of having-mode, not being-mode. Resonance involves *outward* movement—toward relations with others. When resonance occurs in free, loving relations, affection is produced. Affection moves a person out from him or herself towards others, just as God moved to send his one and only Son. Root says, "The source of this sense of connection is not your own self-enclosed affect. It is the *encounter* itself."[27] Through divine encounter and resonance, the church moves outside itself to recognize its relationship. The love of Christ compels the church to live in a constant flow of love with God, each other, and the world. In this way, God's action is manifested in "the fellowship of the Holy Spirit" rather than in the expenditure of energy.

---

25. Root, *Churches and the Crisis*, 167.

26. Root, *Churches and the Crisis*, 211.

27. Root, *Churches and the Crisis*, 168; emphasis in original.

The author says resonance leads to human transformation. As the church encounters the risen Christ, the body of Christ is renewed in his image. In this respect, resonance can even involve suffering. Root observes, "Resonance is a form of action that can directly accompany suffering and bear 'negative' emotion."[28] Negative emotion is not negated in resonance but can lead to instances of encounter. The church is transformed into the image of the crucified Messiah as it suffers in, for, and with Christ. The NT writers understood that suffering in Christ leads to transformation, hope, and glory (Rom 5:3–4; 8:18; Gal 2:20; 6:14; 1 Pet 4:13).

What Can a Church Do?

Considering the crisis of the decline, Root asks, What can churches do? This is where I believe Root's practical ecclesiology falls short. Root outlines a clear diagnosis of the problem facing North American churches today, which the author identifies as the malaise of immanence.[29] Moreover, Root accurately clarifies the church's crisis. Root explains that the North American church's crisis is not a lack of membership or relevance but a failure to see God's action. That is, the crisis of the modern church faces is a failure to see and therefore participate in God's action in the world. However, Root's practical application to guide churches through the crisis falls short of accomplishing his desired outcome, which is life for congregations. Root offers the idea of a "watchword" to lead congregations through this crisis. The author sees watchwords, a term borrowed from the military, as a way for churches to participate in divine action.[30] Root defines *watchword* as "a maxim [or word] that encompasses an individual or group's most central belief or aim."[31] The author understands watchwords as a form of divine action that draws the church's attention to its relations with the world as it waits for God.

28. Root, *Churches and the Crisis*, 169.

29. Charles Taylor calls it "the malaise of immanence" (*Secular Age*, 309).

30. Root, *Churches and the Crisis*, 226.

31. Root, *Churches and the Crisis*, 224–25.

FAITH IN MODERNITY: OUR CULTURAL-THEOLOGICAL CONDITION

Root believes that mainline and evangelical congregations are in crisis not because of dwindling numbers or a loss of social relevance but because "they've avoided a watchword."[32]

As mentioned, Root's suggestion of a watchword is helpful but does not go far enough. Watchwords can help congregations pay attention and wait for God's action, but watchwords are insufficient in *producing the new life forces and forms congregations need*. Watchwords do not address today's congregational malaise of immanence for two reasons. First, watchwords can quickly devolve into another modern management technique or quick fix to help churches grow. In this way, watchwords, like "mission/vision statements," become another form of modern pragmatism. Using watchwords in this way can lead congregations toward a closed construal of the world, thereby restricting God's action. Even Root admits that congregations must find new watchwords once previous ones have run their course. Second, and more importantly, watchwords can diminish the important *relations* by which churches thrive and live. By relying on watchwords, congregations can become more dependent on a technique (or, at worse, a gimmick) than on the *relations* that produce life. As Root often says, churches cannot produce life on their own. Churches that seek life must operate from the very source and foundation of reality, not modern techniques. The only source substantial enough to sustain the church is the person and work of the Holy Spirit (John 6:63). As shown in the next chapter, the Holy Spirit is the Source of life. Through the Spirit, the church of Christ rests in the presence and power of eternal life (John 4:24). Only the Spirit produces what the apostle Paul calls "newness of life" (*kainotes zoes*) (Rom 6:4). This newness of life of the Spirit is different not only in degree but also in kind. It is a new quality of life, a supernatural quality. Churches in the malaise of immanence need a refounding upon the Source of life—the Holy Spirit's presence and power in its midst.[33]

---

32. Root, *Churches and the Crisis*, 224–25.

33. Interestingly, Root identifies the Holy Spirit's essential role in producing life earlier in *Churches and the Crisis*. He writes, "What gives the church life is the gift of participating in this body of Jesus by receiving the Holy Spirit who

A POWERFUL PRESENCE

Bethel Church and the Immanent Frame

The analysis of Charles Taylor and its application to North American churches by Andrew Root sheds light on Bethel Church. Bethel Church is a modern-day, neo-charismatic congregation living inside but not trapped within the immanent frame. The world where Bethel members lived and practiced faith was not a closed universe of causality. Instead, Bethel viewed God's action in a created and open space where moments of divine transcendence and resonance occur and reoccur. God's self-revelation in Christ through the Spirit made transcendence a tangible reality for Bethel members. Bethel's attention to God's presence opened a cavity inside the immanent frame to create space for the Spirit's supernatural activity.

In this way, Bethel's life and ministry reflected the ancient Hebrew story from which the church was named. In Gen 28:10–22, Jacob encounters the God of his fathers while on the run from a revenge-filled brother whom he had wronged. Jacob encounters God historically (in time and space) yet transcendently—in a dream. In the dream, Jacob sees angels ascend and descend upon a ladder. The ladder represents God's action between earth and heaven, assuring Jacob he would be with him on his journey. Upon waking from his dream, Jacob declares, "Surely the Lord is in this place—and I did not know it! . . . How awesome is this place!" (Gen 28:16). Assured of God's presence, Jacob names the place Beth-el, the house of God. Bethel was where God Almighty (Hebrew, *El Shaddai*) encountered his people in power and mystery, transcendence and immanence. Bill Johnson often referenced the story of Jacob in sermons and publications. For Johnson and other Bethel leaders, Jacob's ladder was a paradigm of the Christian faith. Johnson's books, like *Open Heavens* and *When Heaven Meets Earth*, reflect the author's belief that God's

---

is the Spirit of Life. This Holy Spirit, who raised Jesus from the dead, is given to the gathered at Pentecost. The church lives because the same Spirit who raised Jesus from the dead by the will of the Father now lives in the very space of our gathering" (18). However, the author seems to have overlooked this important point in addressing the church's crisis of decline.

58

FAITH IN MODERNITY: OUR CULTURAL-THEOLOGICAL CONDITION

presence and power were available within the immanent frame. Bethel Church aspired to be a house—a ladder—between heaven and earth where God's action ascends and descends.

Consistent with Taylor, the supernatural power evident at Bethel reflected a belief that the human self was porous, not buffered. Bethel members looked to God's power in healing, miracles, and deliverance from oppressive spirits. For example, Scott was a thirty-two-year-old schoolteacher from a southern state who grew up in a Southern Baptist home. Scott moved to Bethel "[because] the power of God was here," he said. Rebecca and Eric Cupp moved to Redding after Rebecca experienced a supernatural healing of her heart valve at a Bethel conference. Kevin, from chapter 1, desired something "more" from his traditional Southern Baptist evangelical church. Kevin had been in torment for years with a chronic stomach ailment before a friend from a "supernatural ministry school" commanded the spirit of infirmity to come out—and it did! Bethel's understanding of the self as *porous* opened members to God's numinous power.

No Crisis of Decline

Per Root's analysis of North American churches, Bethel displayed no crisis of decline. Energy and vitality were in abundance at the church. Enthusiastic worship, long lines of worshippers standing outside the sanctuary doors, and people's willingness to move to Redding, California, were signs of a community teeming with life. Further, Bethel had a robust understanding of God's action in the world. The Holy Spirit facilitated divine encounters of power and transcendence, even within a modern frame. Therefore, instead of being stuck in the malaise of immanence, Bethel flourished and thrived amid life. Bethel did not strategize to accumulate resources or acquire social relevance to beat back decline. Instead, they focused on God's presence in Christ in worship, community life, and spiritual gifts ministry.

A POWERFUL PRESENCE

Resonance at Bethel

If Root is correct that "resonance is life," then this explains why Bethel Church teemed with life. Moments of divine resonance abounded for Bethel members. Resonance occurred through direct encounters with God in Christ mediated by the Spirit. Bethel's expectation of divine encounters opened space for resonance to occur. Through a prophetic word, word of knowledge, healing, or prayer, divine resonance occurred in members' lives, producing spiritual vitality. The unforced dancing, swinging, singing, and emotional manifestations reflected something deep occurring within Bethel members. Bethel was not a program-driven or seeker-sensitive church but a charismatic community focused on God's presence and power. Bethel prioritized being-mode over having-mode through their presence-centered spirituality. Weekend services at Bethel were not curated to attract visitors but for believers to encounter the living God in joy and freedom. As God's presence was highlighted, Bethel members were invited to participate in divine triune life. For example, Robyn was a thirty-something-year-old woman from Taiwan who was initially skeptical of Bethel and its physical manifestations. However, during an unexpected encounter with God during corporate worship, she experienced excessive laughter. As a result of the unusual experience, Robyn was delivered from irrational fears.

Instances of Dissonance

However, despite these moments of divine resonance at Bethel, there were also occasions of dissonance. Spiritual dissonance occurred when Bethel's value for divine presence and being-mode were overshadowed by excessive emotionalism. For example, David, a third-year, twenty-year-old BSSM student, wondered if some BSSM students' excessive manifestations were contrived or "just following the group." Also, John, another BSSM student, wondered if BSSM leaders gave more attention to students or "shiny people" who displayed more physical manifestations. Also, as mentioned

FAITH IN MODERNITY: OUR CULTURAL-THEOLOGICAL CONDITION

in chapter 2, I participated in a group prayer time led by a BSSM third-year student. The third-year student filling in for an absent staff member began the class by enthusiastically announcing, "Okay, today we are going after encounters!" Many in the room cheered and followed the student's lead. The enthusiasm increased across the room as the student leader repeatedly exclaimed, "The fire of God! The fire of God!" As this student led our group prayer, I personally did not sense the Spirit leadership. The student leader and the students' heightened emotional response seemed sudden and forced. The prayer event felt like an occasion of having-mode rather than being-mode. It was an instance where emotionalism replaced genuine affection for Christ. As Andrew Root maintains, Christians move from being-mode to having-mode when emotions are sought for themselves. In this way, Christian spirituality becomes a self-referential and self-enclosed loop, leading to emotional*ism*. In emotionalism, Christian faith loses its dialectic between immanence and transcendence, the earthly and heavenly, and the physical and spiritual. As Root observes, "Life is birthed inside the tension in the dialectic."[34] When Bethel students moved from being-mode to having-mode, divine encounter was lost to emotionalism, and the dialectic collapsed.

34. Root, *Churches and the Crisis*, 211.

Chapter 4

Theological Reflection: The Spirit of Life

The Holy Spirit is the Church's life.—Lesslie Newbigin, *The Household of God*

IN THE NEXT TWO chapters, I open a theological and biblical tradition to interact with Bethel Church and its practice of supernatural power as uncovered in this ethnography. As a pastor sent into a particular context, I understand I carry a theological tradition and interpretation of Scripture that significantly shapes my perception and experience of events. As mentioned, *reflexivity* is the term that ethnographers use to describe one's role in the research and its influence on the results. Further, I acknowledge that my "sentness" carries limitations as well as the potential for new insights. In opening a theological and biblical tradition, I hope for new insights and learnings to emerge for the church in late modernity.

In addition to my own "carried" tradition and interpretation of Scripture, I also considered the perceptions and experiences of local Redding evangelical leaders concerning Bethel. Thankfully, the Redding evangelical leaders I interviewed readily expressed their opinions concerning Bethel. The responses from Redding evangelical leaders reflected a range of sentiments. Some

THEOLOGICAL REFLECTION: THE SPIRIT OF LIFE

leaders expressed support for Bethel, describing their theological agreements while mentioning minor points of dissimilarity or disagreement. Other Evangelicals were neutral, if not indifferent, toward Bethel. For example, these leaders were concerned with some of Bethel's beliefs and practices, such as what they described as Bethel's victorious end-times eschatology or the use of the Passion Translation.[1] However, at the same time, some of these "more neutral" leaders saw a place for Bethel in helping them grow in the "supernatural" ministry, such as healing prayer, deliverance, prophecy, and words of knowledge. And still other Redding Evangelicals I interviewed voiced strong disapproval of Bethel. These Evangelicals questioned Bethel's legitimacy as an evangelical church and declined to partner with them in collaborative ministry efforts. As one senior leader said, "Bethel does not preach the gospel, does not evangelize people, does not get people saved. They know the Holy Spirit; they know emotions, [but] they don't know the saving work of Jesus Christ." Regarding collaborating with Bethel, another Redding pastor said, "We cannot hang the same with [Bethel]. When getting together, we are more likely to say, 'Let's have a Bible study,' and they're more [likely to say], 'What's the Spirit saying?'"

In this chapter, I consider these perspectives as well as my own in exploring Bethel Church's theology of the Spirit and practice of supernatural power. The classic definition of theology first proposed by Anselm is "faith seeking understanding." *Christian theology* is faith in God in the revelation of Jesus Christ, leading to ever-deepening worship and understanding. Professor Daniel Migliore defines theology as "faith asking questions and struggling to find at least provisional answers to these questions."[2] In this score, I examine Bethel's pneumatology, considering the analysis of Jürgen Moltmann and his idea of the Spirit of life.

1. BroadStreet, *Passion Translation*.

2. Migliore, *Faith Seeking Understanding*, 1.

A POWERFUL PRESENCE

Jürgen Moltmann's Theology of the Spirit

Jürgen Moltmann was one of the most prominent theologians of the second half of the twentieth century. In his writings, the German scholar shows particular interest in the person and work of the Holy Spirit. The theme of the Holy Spirit stands large among his works on the Trinity, creation, and ecclesiology.[3] In *The Spirit of Life*, Moltmann presents what he describes as "a holistic pneumatology" that seeks to maintain a Trinitarian framework.[4] Moltmann wants to ensure that God's work of redemption and new creation are held firmly together, understood by the reciprocal relations of the Father, Son, and Holy Spirit. Rather than seeing Christ's ministry as a "one-way street," Moltmann emphasizes the mutuality of the Son and Spirit. The Spirit is not just the operation of the Word but proceeds and determines the Word, even as the Word determines and sends the Spirit. Moltmann says Christ's work is never without the Spirit's work, as the Spirit's work always has Christ's work as its goal. Nonetheless, the Spirit's work is distinguishable from Christ's work. The Spirit's work is neither absorbed by nor replaces Christ's work. The Spirit makes the Son's historical work of redemption accessible to all of creation.

Hebrew Understanding of God's Spirit

Moltmann believes an Old Testament perspective on the Spirit strengthens a proper Trinitarian pneumatology. The author contends that a theology of the Spirit needs to be informed by a *Hebrew* understanding of the Spirit. Moltmann says a continuity exists between God's *ruach* in the OT and the Spirit of Christ in the NT. The author avoids a pneumatology that binds the Spirit solely to the church, either as an institution of mediating grace or official preaching. Moltmann believes that such perspectives impoverish congregations. He argues that the Third Person is not

3. Moltmann: *History and Triune God*; *God in Creation*; *Church in the Power*.

4. Moltmann, *Spirit of Life*, xiii.

64

THEOLOGICAL REFLECTION: THE SPIRIT OF LIFE

only the Spirit of redemption but also the *ruach* of creation and new creation. As the Spirit of new creation, unity exists between the experience of life and the experience of the Spirit. Moltmann believes Western Christianity has been too heavily influenced by Platonic philosophy, which reduces "spirit" to mean disembodied or immaterial. Moltmann contends that the Spirit in the OT is terrestrial and spiritual, material and ethereal, for the ancient Hebrews saw no division between body and spirit.

In the OT, the Holy Spirit is God's divine breath or *ruach*. *Ruach* represents "a tempest, a storm, a force in body and soul, humanity and nature."[5] The concept of *ruach* most likely originated from the Hebrew word for gale or strong wind—a creative force that made the heavens and earth and joined them together. God's *ruach* is closely associated with his word. As in the act of breathing, involving inhaling and exhaling, God's *ruach* is the *breath of his word*. In Exodus, God parts the Red Sea by the *ruach* of his word (14:21). The Psalms see a mutuality between God's word and *ruach*, declaring, "By the word of the Lord the heavens were made, their starry host by the [*ruach*] of his mouth" (Ps 33:6). Because creaturely life was seen in the inhaling and exhaling of air, *ruach* was understood as the breath and power of life (Eccl 3:21; 12:7).[6]

According to Moltmann, there are three dimensions to God's *ruach* in the OT. First, *ruach* is "the confronting event of God's efficacious presence" that reaches the depths of human existence.[7] In Ps 139, the Spirit determines God's presence as David exclaims, "Where can I go from your Spirit? Or where shall I flee from your presence?" (v. 7). Second, God's *ruach* possesses the power of life for all living things. For example, according to Genesis, "Then the Lord God . . . breathed into his nostrils the breath of life, and the man became a living creature" (2:7). Third, God's *ruach* creates the *space* in which life thrives. Psalm 31 declares that God's Spirit is a broad, open space where David breathed

5. Moltmann, *Spirit of Life*, 40.
6. Moltmann, *Spirit of Life*, 41.
7. Moltmann, *Spirit of Life*, 42.

life again.[8] David says, "And you have not delivered me into the hand of the enemy; you have set my feet in a broad place" (v. 8). Moltmann says *ruach* "leads us out of narrow places into wide vistas, thus conferring life."[9]

The Spirit of Life

Moltmann sees the Spirit in the OT as the Spirit of life. The Spirit is "holy" because he sanctifies life and renews the face of the earth (Ps 104:30).[10] The Spirit in the OT is "the life-force of created beings and the living space in which they can grow and develop their potentialities."[11] "The Spirit sets this life in the presence of the living God and in the great river of eternal love."[12] Moltmann argues against false dichotomies that view divine revelation over against human experience, found prominently within Western Christianity. The early church fathers, especially Augustine, mistakenly divided between body and soul and the physical and spiritual. By reducing Christian faith to one's "soul's quest for God," Augustine created an unnecessary dualism between sensory and spiritual experiences. Moltmann offers a more *Hebrew* understanding of the Spirit and human experience, one that unifies divine action and the human senses. He presents a spirituality where one is not looking to leave behind the body (or society) to be with God. The author says we experience God, other people, and creation *through the body*—that is, through our senses. Moltmann does not seek to separate from the world in order to escape it. Moltmann recognizes the Spirit as the source of life in all of creation. He writes, "The eternal Spirit is the divine wellspring of life—the source of life created, life preserved and life daily renewed, and finally the

---

8. Moltmann, *Spirit of Life*, 42.

9. Moltmann, *Spirit of Life*, 43.

10. Moltmann, *Spirit of Life*, 8.

11. Moltmann, *Spirit of Life*, 84.

12. Moltmann, *Spirit of Life*, x.

THEOLOGICAL REFLECTION: THE SPIRIT OF LIFE

source of eternal life of all created being."[13] The experience of life in Christ is the experience of God.

Immanent Transcendence

An essential aspect of Moltmann's pneumatology is his understanding of the Spirit's "immanent transcendence."[14] Immanent transcendence is Moltmann's response to Barth and the other dialectical theologians who posited a theology "from above" that drew a "thick line" between immanence and transcendence or the world's givenness and non-givenness.[15] Moltmann does not see revelation and human experience as antitheses but understands the Spirit as immanently transcendent in everyday life. In Christ, "it is therefore possible to experience God *in, with and beneath* each everyday experience of the world, if God is in all things, and if all things are in God, so that God himself 'experiences' all things in his own way."[16] For Moltmann, the Spirit is known in the self, in relationships ("sociality"), and nature. He says that because God's Spirit is present in human beings, the human spirit is "self-transcendently aligned toward God."[17] Through the Spirit, God is transcendently present in everyday human experiences.

Moltmann's understanding of God as Creator is the foundation of his concept of immanent transcendence. In creation, God breathed his own Spirit into all living things. Therefore, there is no division between the earthly and heavenly, spirit and body. Moltmann says the doctrine of creation "already invokes the idea of immanent transcendence."[18] The Spirit is the power of creation and the wellspring of life; nonetheless, the Spirit is distinct

13. Moltmann, *Spirit of Life*, 82.

14. Moltmann, *Spirit of Life*, 31–38.

15. Barth and other dialectical theologians were reacting to Schleiermacher's idea of "immediate self-consciousness" where the Spirit was imbued within human conscience (Moltmann, *Spirit of Life*, 32).

16. Moltmann, *Spirit of Life*, 34; emphasis in original.

17. Moltmann, *Spirit of Life*, 7.

18. Moltmann, *Spirit of Life*, 37.

from creation. Moltmann believes that immanent transcendence explains human beings in their *totality*—body and soul, conscious and unconscious, and personality and sociality. Immanent transcendence also accounts for creation's *wholeness*, as humanity and creation share in organic and spiritual life together.[19] Moltmann's vision of the Spirit's immanent transcendence reunifies what modernity sought to divide: the natural world from divine presence and action.

NT Spirit Christology

In *The Spirit of Life*, Moltmann turns his attention to the NT, arguing that a proper pneumatology is impossible without first accounting for *Jesus's experience of the Spirit*. The author puts forward a *Spirit Christology* to clarify the early church's experience of the Spirit. Moltmann's Spirit Christology is based on Jesus's history with the Spirit as described in the Gospels. He observes that the Synoptic Gospels begin with a Spirit Christology, whereas Paul and John have it as their premise.[20] Spirit Christology compliments—but does not replace—Logos Christology. Logos Christology emphasizes Jesus as the Divine Word becoming flesh, whereas Spirit Christology emphasizes Jesus's *humanity as filled with the Spirit*.[21] Moltmann says that Spirit Christology sees "the historical Jesus's himself in theological terms, as God's messiah child, the Spirit-imbued human being who comes from the Spirit, is led by the Spirit, acts and ministers in the Spirit, and through the Spirit surrenders himself to death on a cross."[22] Spirit Christology recognizes Jesus *as a man of the Spirit* who sends the Spirit following his resurrection.

---

19. Moltmann presents a strong theological case for ecology (*Source of Life*, 111–22). For his full theology of creation, see *God in Creation*.

20. Moltmann, *Spirit of Life*, 58.

21. Clark Pinnock says Logos Christology addresses the person of Jesus, while Spirit Christology addresses his work (*Flame of Love*, 91–92).

22. Moltmann, *Spirit of Life*, 58.

Moltmann contends that Logos Christology has dominated the Western landscape since the inclusion of *filioque* (and the Son—meaning that the Holy Spirit proceeds from both the Father and the Son) in the Nicene Creed in AD 1054. Moltmann sees the church's addition of *filioque* as superfluous, an unnecessary inclusion. At the time, the church rightly understood the Spirit as being sent by the Son but not proceeding from him. However, *filioque* led the Latinized world to see the Spirit *as subordinate to the Son*. Moltmann argues that *filioque* positioned the Son ahead of the Spirit—even subordinate from its very origin.[23]

The Spirit of Christ in the Church

In his pneumatology, Moltmann distinguishes between Jesus's experience of the Spirit (Spirit Christology) and the church's experience of the Spirit of Christ (christological pneumatology). Christological pneumatology is found primarily in Paul's and John's writings. The author says that Jesus's experience of the Spirit and the church's experience of the Spirit of Christ are not contradictory but complimentary, existing in mutual relationship and interpretation. Moltmann argues, "It is important to stress both sides here. Christian faith is a response to the word of the messianic gospel and the resonance of that word in the hearts and lives of men and women."[24] According to Paul, Jesus "became a life-giving spirit" following his life, death, and resurrection (1 Cor 15:45). Jesus's resurrection and ascension marked the transitional moment when the Christ of the Spirit became the Spirit of Christ for the church. The Holy Spirit accompanied Jesus in his death, raising him again and uniting with him in his ascension.

---

23. Moltmann says that the Western Church largely ignored and resisted the mutual relationship between the Son and Spirit following the *filioque* inclusion. He writes, "Recognition of the substantially determined mutual relationship between the pneumatological christology of the synoptics in the christological pneumatology of Paul and John was largely ignored in the traditions of the Western church. And approaches to the Spirit christology in the movements for Christian reform were actually resisted" (*Spirit of Life*, 59).

24. Moltmann, *Spirit of Life*, 68.

In view of this transition, Jesus informed his disciples that it was better for him to go away so that the Advocate would come (John 16:7). Moltmann argues for a perichoretic structure to the Son and Spirit existing and working together—*in one another.* Therefore, Moltmann avoids the pitfalls of some liberation theologies that view the Spirit as independent from the Word. Moltmann argues for a relative independence of the Spirit.

Moltmann sees the mutual relations of the Son and Spirit as the key to the church's kerygma. The Spirit by which the church confesses, "Jesus is Lord!" *is the Spirit of the resurrected Christ and Yahweh's ruach.* Moltmann says the church's union with God is experienced "in the Spirit" and has Christ as its sole lodestone.[25] He writes, "The experience of the Spirit makes Christ—the *risen* Christ—present, and with him make the eschatological future present too."[26]

The Spirit Liberates for Life

For Moltmann, the experience of God's Spirit is the experience of liberation. He defines liberation as "being set free for life."[27] The work of the Spirit encompasses inward and outward possibilities involving personal, social, and political liberation. The Spirit's power is transcendent in its foundation, providing inexhaustible energies for its immanent work. Moltmann sees the Spirit's liberation represented in both Testaments. In the OT, Exodus depicts God delivering his people from the bondage of slavery and into the land of liberty. Through the exodus event, God reveals himself as "Lord/Yahweh" who saves his people from their oppressors. Moltmann writes,

> To say God is Lord means: "God is *the liberator*.["] So God's rule means the wide, *free space* he gives for the freedom of his people. God's power manifests itself in

25. Moltmann, *Spirit of Life*, 68.
26. Moltmann, *Spirit of Life*, 147; emphasis in original.
27. Moltmann, *Spirit of Life*, 99.

THEOLOGICAL REFLECTION: THE SPIRIT OF LIFE

"the strong arm" with which he delivers his people from slavery and saves them from their armed pursuers; so we can call it *free power*. To believe in God means trusting his promise and his guidance, and experiencing one's own liberations.[28]

In the NT, Yahweh is the Father of the Lord Jesus Christ, who delivered the Israelites from slavery. God's liberation begins with Jesus's anointing by the Spirit. The NT writers present Messiah Jesus as the "Lord of the OT" who sets God's people free from death. Those who follow Jesus are delivered from sickness, demonic possession, and social and religious humiliation. The NT presents Yahweh as the God of the crucified Jesus, the victim of power. The Spirit is the liberating energy that raised Jesus from the dead and gave him eternal life. The NT defines God as the one "who raised Christ Jesus from the dead," who liberated him from death (Rom 10:9–10).[29] The OT exodus and the NT resurrection are paradigmatic stories of God liberating his people from the powers of sin.

For the apostle Paul, Jesus's liberation is conferred to the church via the Spirit. Moltmann says Jesus's resurrection is the framework by which Yahweh expands history. The Spirit of Christ creates new energies of life through the word of the gospel. The Spirit and Word work together to generate kairos moments of God's action. Moltmann argues that having the Word alone is insufficient; the Word and Spirit work together to open new possibilities. Moltmann writes, "If the workings of the Holy Spirit are seen only as the subjective operation of the objective word of God in the hearts of believers, they are being too narrowly defined."[30] Moltmann argues that Word and Spirit work together in human life and creation to bring about inward and outward possibilities.

---

28. Moltmann, *Spirit of Life*, 100; emphasis in original.

29. Moltmann, *Spirit of Life*, 101.

30. Moltmann, *Spirit of Life*, 103.

A POWERFUL PRESENCE

Pneumatic Ecclesiology for God's People

Drawing from Moltmann's theology of the Spirit, Terry Cross presents an understanding of the Spirit in forming Christian *and* Christian communities. Cross offers a theology of the church with what he calls a pneumatic ecclesiology. According to Cross, pneumatic Christology highlights

> the role of the Spirit in creating believers who are new creatures in Christ; in grafting us into the body of Christ, his church; in shaping this new community into the likeness of Christ; and in constituting this new community with such love, unity, and power that the *missio Dei* (mission of God) is being fulfilled in this world by its action.[31]

Cross's pneumatic ecclesiology holds exciting possibilities for how the church understands its identity and call.

Pneumatic ecclesiology is reflected in the NT image of the church as "the people of God." The NT uses several images to describe the church (e.g., the body of Christ, the bride of Christ, the temple of the Holy Spirit, etc.), but the church as "the people of God's presence" is especially helpful for a postindustrial, capitalistic society. The church as "a people" is a radical departure from the common view of the church as a *place where things happen*. According to this modern view—which has persisted since the Reformation—the church is understood as *a building where religious activities occur*. Because of the influence of hyper-capitalism, the American version of this sees the church as a vendor of spiritual goods and services. However, the church as "the people of God's presence" recaptures a redemptive, holistic vision of Christ's body. The image of "the people of God" is also the most extensively used image of the church in Scripture, represented in both Testaments (Deut 4:10; 31:30; Matt 16:18; Eph 1:22).[32]

The church as "the people of God's presence" highlights three vital aspects of Christ's body, identified by three catchwords: people, presence, and power. First, a pneumatic ecclesiology sees

31. Cross, *People of God's Presence*, 7.

32. Ryken et al., "Church."

THEOLOGICAL REFLECTION: THE SPIRIT OF LIFE

the church *as a people* or a community. The church is a people elected and formed by God from out of all the world's peoples. For example, Moses reminds the Israelites of their identity as God's *especially loved people*. Moses says, "The Lord your God has chosen you out of all the people on the face of the earth to be his people, his treasured possession" (Deut 7:6). In the NT, Peter reminds his primarily gentile audience, "Once you were not a people, but now you are the people of God" (1 Pet 2:10). In both old and new covenants, God creates, sustains, and forms his people by his Spirit (Exod 13:2; Ps 104:30; Acts 2:1–4; Gal 3:5).

Second, a pneumatic ecclesiology sees the church as the people of *God's presence*. God personally dwells with his people in Christ via the Spirit. For example, during the exodus, God's presence moves from Mt. Sinai to the tabernacle and to the promised land to be with his people. At Pentecost, God's presence rests upon those gathered in the upper room (Acts 2:4).[33] The events of Pentecost were similar to the Israelites' experience of Yahweh at Mt. Sinai. At Pentecost, Jesus's 120 followers experienced rushing wind, thunderous sound, and burning fire. The people of God experience God *directly and evidentially* through the Spirit. Although many ecclesiologies view God's presence as mediated through various avenues of grace or official preaching, a pneumatic ecclesiology holds that God is present *directly*. Therefore, God and man have no special mediator other than the Spirit of the risen Christ. The unmediated union between Christ and his people occurs Spirit to spirit (Rom 8:16). Also, a pneumatic ecclesiology holds Christian spirituality and ethics firmly together since the Spirit's fruit is love (Gal 5:16–26). The church lives in the presence and power of the resurrected Christ as it serves in faith, hope, and love.

Third, the people of God's presence are a circle of *divine power*. God's resurrection power is manifested in the gathered space of his people as he nurtures, empowers, and guides them. God's people are unleashed through the Spirit in worship,

33. Craig Keener notes that the description of the disciples being "filled with the Spirit" is Luke's way of showing Pentecost's continuity with the OT prophets (*Acts*, 1:806).

ministry, and mission. In this way, mission is best understood as *extending God's presence to the world.* God confers his power and authority upon the church via the Spirit for its life and mission. Cross observes, "It is the Spirit of God who brings into our finite, sinful world a direct encounter with God's presence and power so that the new community formed by God's hand continues the ministry of Christ here and now."[34]

The Ministry of God's People

A pneumatic ecclesiology shapes how the church practices ministry. Here we define *ministry* as the service in and among the body of Christ. As "the people of God's presence," members serve primarily through spiritual gifts. God manifests his powerful presence through spiritual gifts (or charismata). Paul says, "All these [spiritual gifts] are empowered by one and the same Spirit, who apportions to each one individually as he wills" (1 Cor 12:11). The spiritual gifts are a direct form of God's action. The spiritual gifts mentioned in 1 Cor 12 and elsewhere are functional in character, not hierarchal. The charismata do not refer to a member's "personal attributes" or "ministerial offices" but *specific actions of the Spirit in the church.* Further, these spiritual gifts are given to each member (v. 7). As Cross observes, there is a radical spiritual egalitarianism to the Spirit.[35] Spiritual gifts also shape how leadership is exercised. Even the "leadership gifts" of Eph 4:11 are functional in shape. For example, "apostles, prophets, evangelists, pastors, and teachers" demonstrate an increased measure of the Spirit's anointing in those respective areas. Since the charismata are functional, charismatic leadership does not operate from a place of hierarchy but equality. In this score, women have an essential role in the church and in ministry. Since all people are empowered with charismata, then all can serve. The NT shows that women are vital to

---

34. Cross, *People of God's Presence*, 7.
35. Cross, *People of God's Presence*, 113.

THEOLOGICAL REFLECTION: THE SPIRIT OF LIFE

ministry (Acts 2:1–4) and perform crucial services in the church's mission (Acts 21:4; Rom 16:3–15; Phil 4:2).

A Kingdom of Priests

Cross says that when the church serves in its charismatic capacities, it represents "a kingdom of priests."[36] In both the Old and New Testaments, God's people are considered a royal priesthood who serve before God's presence (Exod 19:6; 1 Pet 2:5, 9; Rev 1:6). Martin Luther described the nonclerical nature of the church as "the priesthood of all believers." Old Testament priests worshipped at the altar by offering God animal and other sacrifices. In the NT, Jesus is the great High Priest who made one sacrifice for sin, once and for all (Heb 4:14; 10:10).[37] Jesus's sacrifice opened unmediated access to God's throne of grace (Heb 4:16). In God's house, brothers and sisters follow Jesus, their elder brother, in his royal priestly line.[38] The church as a royal priesthood offers sacrifices of worship, praise, and confession (Rom 12:1–2; Heb 13:15–16). Many evangelical structures today unintentionally erect an ecclesial caste system by requiring ordination or advanced degrees for its ministers. Such distinctions widen the clergy/laity divide. However, the NT picture of the church is that every member is a minister through spiritual gifts.

Mission as the People of God

Finally, pneumatic ecclesiology shapes the church's mission to the world. Here, the "people of God's presence" are sent to embody Christ's reign to the nations. In this way, the church serves as a hermeneutic of the gospel, allowing the world to interpret Christ's presence and power amid human weakness.[39] The Spirit

36. Cross, *People of God's Presence*, 26.
37. Ellingworth, "Priests."
38. Cross, *Serving the People*, 29.
39. Newbigin, *Gospel in Pluralist Society*, 222–33.

A POWERFUL PRESENCE

is central to the church's mission. God's Spirit initiates, directs, and equips the church people to carry the gospel of Christ in power and to the ends of the earth (Acts 1:8, 13:3). Interestingly, Paul understands his own mission not as "the ministry of justification by faith" or "the mission of the church" but as "the ministry of the Spirit" (2 Cor 3:8).

As participants in God's mission, the body of Christ does not rely primarily on methods, programs, or "missional principles" but on the Spirit's intuition, direction, and power. Paul understood that God uses the ordinary and foolish to shame the wise (1 Cor 1:27). God equips the church with the Spirit's fruits and gifts in his missional enterprise. The fruit of the Spirit offers an alternative reality and social order to the world's system of fear and domination. The spirit given to the church is *the Spirit of holiness*. God's people embody Christ's goodness and justice in the world in the power of the Spirit. As the church worships God, fellowships in the Spirit (*koinonia*), and proclaims Christ (*kerygma*), discipleship (*diakonia*) leads to faithful witness in the world (*marturia*).

The spiritual gifts can also lead to evangelism. For example, Paul encourages the Corinthians to remember the "unbelievers and outsiders" who may be present in their congregation (1 Cor 14:24). He therefore instructs the church to prophesy rather than speak in tongues due to prophecy's revelatory nature. He writes, "But if all prophesy, and an unbeliever or outsider enters, he is convicted by all, he is called to account by all" (v. 24). Paul understood that prophecy could lead to the conversion of an unbeliever, saying, "Falling on his face, he will worship God and declare that God is really among you" (v. 26). In Acts, Luke records how the ecstatic behavior of the church served to advance the gospel (Acts 2; 10; 19:11). The gifts of the Spirit were instrumental in the early church's growth in Acts. As Luke highlights, "Many signs and wonders were regularly done among the people by the hands of the apostles" (Acts 5:12).

THEOLOGICAL REFLECTION: THE SPIRIT OF LIFE

Bethel Church in Theological Perspective

In this section, we reflect upon Moltmann and Cross's theological analysis above, considering Bethel Church and its practice of supernatural power. Here I make three observations. First, Bethel's pneumatology reflects Moltmann's understanding of the Spirit as the *ruach* of life. Second, Bethel's Spirit Christology is the key to understanding its faith and ministry of supernatural power. Finally, though bountiful, Bethel's spirituality or life in the Spirit is challenged to preserve a christological focus in moments of heightened spiritual enthusiasm.

The Spirit of Life at Bethel

Jürgen Moltmann's understanding of the Spirit of life provides insight into Bethel's pneumatology and spiritual practice. Bethel sees the Holy Spirit as God's *ruach*, the divine breath of life who produces life and power for his creation. The Spirit is the *ruach* of redemption *and* new creation. Bill Johnson's frequent preaching from the OT reflected this Hebraic emphasis. Johnson often preached from the Genesis, Exodus, Psalms, and the Prophets to highlight God's *ruach* filling creation and his people with divine life and power. According to Bethel, the charismatic figures of Judges were flawed but Spirit-empowered leaders to emulate due to their reliance upon the Spirit. Ezekiel's vision of God breathing life into the valley of dry bones was a paradigmatic picture of a NT reality of the Spirit's arrival (Ezek 36–37). Bethel viewed the Holy Spirit as the divine breath of life that makes all things new in Christ.

Because of Bethel's emphasis on the Spirit, life and vitality were abundant at the church. Bethel's spiritual vitality was evident in their passionate worship, extensive ministry, and testimonies of God's powerful action involving healings and deliverances. The Spirit facilitated unmediated divine encounters, which produced life and energy for members. For example, men and women, boys and girls moved and danced enthusiastically during praise and worship. Long lines of worshippers formed outside the sanctuary doors as people sought direct encounters with the living God. People were willing to travel from around the world to experience God's dynamic power at the church. Bethel's view of the Spirit corresponded to Moltmann's: "The eternal Spirit is the divine wellspring of life—the source of life created, life preserved and life daily renewed, and finally the source of eternal life of all created being."[40] Bethel's understanding of the Spirit created a holistic vision of faith and life as the divine *ruach* was the Spirit of redemption and resurrected life.

Bethel's Spirit theology reflected Moltmann's description of the Spirit as immanent transcendence. The church's presence-centered spirituality allowed supernatural encounters to occur in a modern context. These encounters were not restricted to the official preaching of the church or the sacraments, but they were experienced directly—via the Holy Spirit. The unmediated access to God enlivened worship, group prayer, or members' experiences of creation. The spiritual gifts (charismata) produced energies of life. God's transcendent action was immanently manifested through a prophetic word, a word of knowledge, or healing prayer. Ministry within the church or mission to the world was fueled by a belief that God was present and active even in a causal world. Personal testimonies of God's supernatural power from Bethel members highlighted the unity between divine immanence and transcendence. The Holy Spirit was a non-reductive and evidential reality at Bethel.

Bethel's understanding of the Spirit as a divine *ruach* (or holy *pneuma*) was also a source of liberation for church members. Testimonies abounded at Bethel of people's personal, emotional, spiritual, and physical freedom from unwanted thoughts, behaviors, attractions, or oppressive spirits. To Bethel members, nothing was impossible for God. For example, Rebecca Cupp experienced liberation from a faulty heart valve, Kevin experienced freedom from a chronic stomach ailment, and Robyn was delivered from irrational fears. The Spirit made Christ's work on the restoration accessible to Bethel members' spiritual, physical, and

40. Moltmann, *Spirit of Life*, 82.

emotional pain. Such Spirit-empowered relief and restoration led to personal and social liberation.

A Strong Spirit Christology

Bethel's supernatural approach was informed by its Spirit Christology. Bethel affirmed a Logos Christology but emphasized Spirit Christology, seeing Jesus as a man anointed by God's Spirit. Understanding Jesus as "a man of the Spirit" empowered Bethel members to follow in Jesus's natural/supernatural footsteps. Bethel's Spirit Christology shaped members' expectations of serving as a channel of divine power and grace. To some conservative Evangelicals, Bethel's attention to the Spirit seemed to lack a proper Christology. For example, one evangelical Redding pastor said of Bethel, "They are stuck on: Holy Spirit, Holy Spirit, Holy Spirit." However, Bethel regularly affirmed Christ's divine nature and work in its worship, teaching, and ministry. Considering Moltmann's analysis that the Son and Spirit work mutually and reciprocally together, Bethel held to a robust pneumatology that informed its worship and service. In most instances, Bethel's attention to the Spirit existed within a christological and Trinitarian framework.

Bethel's Spirit Christology led the church to practice a pneumatic ecclesiology ("a people of God's presence"). As Cross explains, pneumatic ecclesiology highlights the role of the Spirit in creating new persons in Christ and sending the church out on mission with power. Bethel's pneumatic ecclesiology was reflected in its presence-centered spirituality, where the church operated as the "people of God's presence." Rather than seeing the church as a vendor of religious goods and services or a place where religious activities occur (to attract new members), Bethel understood themselves *as the people* of God where God's Spirit dwells personally. Considering its pneumatic ecclesiology identity, Bethel was concerned with growing not a big church but "big people." Bethel focused on "hosting God's presence" rather than attracting religious consumers.

A POWERFUL PRESENCE

As a fellowship *of the Spirit*, spiritual gifts became the primary means of serving others and manifesting God's numinous power. Through prophetic words, words of knowledge, worship, and preaching, men and women, boys and girls served as "royal priests." As a royal priesthood, Bethel members were empowered to serve others with gifts of faith, healing, miracles, and inspired words. The ministry as a royal priesthood occurred inside and outside the church. These Spirit ministries opened new pathways for unbelievers to see and experience God's action.

Every Bethel member understood they were equipped with spiritual gifts and was encouraged to use them. Spiritual gifts were functional in character, creating a nonhierarchical environment at the church. Spiritual gifts empowered men *and women* to serve in prominent leadership positions. For example, women served as apostles, prophets, evangelists, pastors, teachers, and other influential positions. Women were empowered to serve because they, too, were anointed by the Holy Spirit.

Spirituality Without Christ?

However, considering the above correspondence with Moltmann and Cross, there was an area of Bethel's faith and practice at variance with the above analysis. As mentioned, Moltmann aimed to maintain a Trinitarian framework in his understanding of the Holy Spirit. Moltmann holds that the Spirit and Son exist in mutual relations and that the work of the Spirit has the work of Christ as its goal. In other words, the Spirit sent by the Father works in a christological direction. While at Bethel, there were instances when I wondered if members' spiritual enthusiasm held to this Trinitarian framework and christological focus. For example, on a few occasions of heightened enthusiasm, it seemed that Bethel members lost sight of the person and presence of Christ. Here, I draw from the example mentioned in chapter 3, where I participated in a prayer group led by a BSSM third-year student. The third-year student, filling in for an absent staff member, opened the prayer meeting by announcing, "Okay, today we are going after encounters!" Then

80

THEOLOGICAL REFLECTION: THE SPIRIT OF LIFE

many in the room followed the student's lead, cheering and praying loudly. As mentioned, the sudden rise of energy and emotion (in the previously quiet) room seemed forced, if not self-referential. As a participant observer, the goal of the prayer meeting seemed to be "spiritual enthusiasm" rather than communion with Christ. On this occasion, it seemed as if enthusiasm was the goal, not Christ. According to Moltmann, spiritual enthusiasm that lacks a christological center does not lead to *life*. As Jesus explains, life is found in him through the Spirit (John 6:63; 14:6). Bethel leaders would be well served to keep the person and presence of Christ in view during occasions of heightened enthusiasm.

As Moltmann observes, the presence of the Holy Spirit is also *the Spirit of Christ* in the church (1 Cor 15:45; Phil 1:19). In this way, Bethel's experience of the Spirit would also involve participation in the risen Christ, thereby holding to a Trinitarian framework even during intense occasions of enthusiasm. If evangelical churches must work to avoid Christomonism, then charismatic and Pentecostal churches like Bethel must work to prevent pneumonism. By keeping Christ the goal of enthusiasm, Bethel's life in the Spirit will also be discipleship with Jesus.[41]

---

41. Exalting Christ in spiritual encounters also leads to what Scot McKnight calls "Christoformity." Christoformity is the process by which God forms his people in and through Jesus's life, death, resurrection, and ascension. In Christoformity, God's people are transformed into Christ's likeness, reflecting the Spirit's fruits like love, joy, peace, patience, kindness, goodness, faithfulness, gentleness, and self-control (Gal 5:22–23) (McKnight, *Pastor Paul*).

Chapter 5

Biblical and Exegetical Analysis: Eschatological Enthusiasm

> God is revealed to have limitless power and resources; He regularly shows Himself strong on behalf of His People. Yet His people still live out their redeemed lives in a fallen world, where the whole creation, including the human body, is in "bondage to decay" (Rom 8:21), and will continue to be so until we receive "the redemption of our bodies" (8:23).—
> Gordon Fee, *The Disease of Health and Wealth Gospels*

As CHAPTER 4 MENTIONED, locating one's theological point of view and interpretation of Scripture is essential when opening a theological tradition. As an Evangelical, I am grounded in the theological conviction that personal, born-again faith and conversion are necessary for salvation, personal holiness is essential to Christian faithfulness, and the Scriptures are God's inspired and authoritative word. The Bible declares the good news of the arrival of God's kingdom culminating in his Son, Jesus Christ, in the power of the Spirit (2 Tim 3:16). For the church in modernity, the Bible does not serve as a canon of propositional truths in which to build a foundation of scientific certainty (or what has been called *foundationalism*).

BIBLICAL AND EXEGETICAL ANALYSIS: ESCHATOLOGICAL ENTHUSIASM

Although Scripture possesses propositional content, it consists of various genres and forms, such as history, poetry, wisdom, promise, and warning, that cannot be reduced to mere propositions. Also, the Bible is not a system of theological ideas or moral values. It is not a theological textbook. Further, the Bible does not work as an "identity narrative" that derives its ultimate meaning and authority from the church's life and language. In contrast to these views, I see the Bible as *the word of God*—that is, divine speech in action. As such, the Bible derives its authority on its own terms. As *God's* word, it becomes the source of authoritative teaching and sound doctrine of the church. Scripture serves as the norm of the church and a source of life and vitality.

From Text to Context

As a pastor entering a new setting, I seek to understand the Bible in its original context and see the local context *through* Scripture. The task of the contextual theologian is to move from the text (exegesis) to interpreting the local situation through what God is doing there as revealed in Scripture (hermeneutics). Following Kevin Vanhoozer, I understand Scripture as a theo-drama or "script" by which the church participates in God's unfolding word and action in the world.[1] This divinely inspired script, or Scripture, reveals God's testimonies and speech-acts. As speech-act, the Bible does not merely impart information about God, salvation, or the end-times but speaks and enacts promises, assurances, and the fullness of salvation in Christ through the Spirit. When read this way, coupled with faith in the light of Christ, the Bible has life-giving, sacramental power. As an Evangelical entering a new context, I therefore looked to understand Bethel Church according to the word of God. Through appreciative conversations with Bethel members and leaders—in view of Scripture—I opened space for pastoral dialogue to occur.

1. Vanhoozer, *Drama of Doctrine*.

A POWERFUL PRESENCE

James Dunn and the Early Church

In this score, James D. G. Dunn is a helpful conversation partner in clarifying Bethel Church and its practice of supernatural power. Dunn was a longtime professor of divinity at the University of Durham and a prolific writer in New Testament studies. In *Jesus and the Spirit*, he examines the charismatic experiences of Jesus and the early Christians, as evidenced in the Gospels, the book of Acts, and Paul's writings. For Dunn, the NT writings reveal the experiential basis of early Christianity. He writes, "Their gospel was in large measure the expression of their experience."[2] Dunn believes that the experiential dimension of Jesus and the early church's faith is determinative for later Christianity. Dunn also contends that the early Christian experience was shaped significantly by the anticipation of Jesus's return. He says Christianity began as an enthusiastic sect within first-century Judaism that was apocalyptic in character. "Eschatological enthusiasm" is the phrase Dunn employs to describe first-century Christian faith. He writes, "In short, their experience of the Spirit was such that they could not doubt that they were in the last days, that the salvation history of God was reaching its climax and consummation."[3]

Jesus's Charismatic Experience (Gospels)

Dunn argues that the Gospels demonstrate how Jesus lived and ministered from his dual role as God's Son *and* the Anointed One of the Spirit. However, it was from this latter identity—his anointing by the Spirit—that Jesus was empowered for ministry. Dunn writes, "Jesus thought of himself as God's son and anointed by the eschatological Spirit, because in prayer he experienced God as Father and in the ministry he experienced a power to heal which he could only understand as the power of the end-time . . . [and] the gospel of the end-time."[4] The dynamic power at work in

2. Dunn, *Jesus and the Spirit*, 13.

3. Dunn, *Jesus and the Spirit*, 163.

4. Dunn, *Jesus and the Spirit*, 67.

84

Jesus occurred through the Spirit and was a present sign of God's future kingdom.

Was Jesus a Charismatic?

In *Jesus and the Spirit,* Dunn explores the provocative question *Was Jesus a charismatic?* The question has bearing upon the kind of faith Jesus practiced and its continuity with the early church. Dunn explores the question of Jesus's charismatic character in three ways: Jesus the miracle worker, Jesus's divine authority, and Jesus's ministry as a prophet.

First, Dunn understands Jesus's reputation as a miracle worker explicitly in *charismatic terms.* In the Gospels, Jesus demonstrates unparalleled *dunameis* or "mighty works." In Luke's account in Acts the early church understood Jesus as "a man attested . . . by mighty works" (Acts 2:22). To a first-century audience, Jesus's miracle-working ability authenticated him as a person of the Spirit (Acts 2:22; Matt 11:21; Mark 6:2; Gal 3:5; 2 Cor 12:12). Dunn writes, "In Hellenistic circles at least the working of *dunameis* belonged to the charismata, a manifestation of the Spirit (1 Cor. 12.10, 28f.)."[5] Through divine *dunameis,* Jesus caused the blind to see, the deaf to hear, and the lame to walk. Jesus's mighty works even involved power over nature, such as feeding multitudes, walking on water, and calming a storm.

Second, Jesus exercised unprecedented authority (*exousia*) through his teaching and exorcisms. On one occasion, Jesus delivers a man from demonic influence while teaching in a synagogue in Capernaum. Jesus delivers the man simply by commanding the demon to come out. Mark says that those who witnessed the event were "amazed" at Jesus's power (Mark 1:27). The crowd responds by saying, "What is this? A new teaching with authority! He commands even the unclean spirits, and they obey him" (Mark 1:27). Jesus's authority to heal the sick and deliver the demonized

---

5. Dunn, *Jesus and the Spirit,* 70.

A POWERFUL PRESENCE

extended to him forgiving others' sins (Mark 2:11). Dunn describes Jesus's *exousia* as "the immediate authority of God."[6]

Finally, in the Gospels, Jesus was considered a prophet who possessed the Spirit of God. Jesus is referred to as a prophet throughout the Synoptic Gospels (Mark 6:15; 8:28; 14:65; Matt 21:11, 46; Luke 7:16, 39; 24:19). Dunn says that Jesus's reputation as a prophet is even more striking considering that the gift of prophecy had ceased during the Second Temple Judean exile period. Jesus refers to himself as a prophet, stating, "A prophet is not without honor, except in his hometown and among his relatives and in his own household" (Mark 6:4). Further, Jesus displayed the characteristics of a prophet by providing divine insight (Matt 9:4), foreseeing future events (Luke 19:31), and even predicting the manner of his death and resurrection (Matt 16:21).

In exploring *Was Jesus a charismatic?* Dunn says there is no evidence that Jesus demonstrated *ecstatic Christianity*. Ecstatic Christianity involves "an unusually exalted state of feeling, a condition of such total absorption or concentration that the individual becomes oblivious to all attendant circumstances and other stimuli, an experience of intense rapture or a trance-like state in which normal formal faculties are suspended."[7] Although Luke depicts Jesus experiencing enthusiasm in the Spirit (10:21), the Gospels never mention Jesus, for example, speaking in tongues or being taken up in ecstatic experiences.

The Charismatic Experience of the Early Church (Acts)

In *Jesus and the Spirit*, Dunn turns his attention to the charismatic experience of the early church evidenced in Acts. Acts details how the church was conceived and grew during its infancy. Acts demonstrates how the early church was enlivened through supernatural phenomena and ecstatic experiences. The story of Acts is a fulfillment of Jesus's promise that the church will receive power

6. Dunn, *Jesus and the Spirit*, 79.
7. Dunn, *Jesus and the Spirit*, 84.

86

(dunamis) to be his witnesses throughout the earth (1:8). Dunn says, "[The] earliest Christian community was essentially charismatic and enthusiastic in nature, in every aspect of its common life and worship, its development and mission."[8] The church in Acts was charismatic in four areas: Pentecost, prophetic speech, supernatural mission, and the gift of the Spirit.

First, the book of Acts begins with the curious event of Pentecost, where Jesus's disciples were baptized with the fire of the Holy Spirit. One hundred twenty followers of Jesus were gathered in the upper room in Jerusalem, apparently waiting for Jesus's return. There, they experienced a vibro-acoustic heavenly event consisting of loud rushing wind and blazing tongues of fire. The descending tongues of fire then separated and rested on everyone in the room. The event of Pentecost was experiential in character, as the gathered disciples *heard* the sound, *felt* the wind, and *saw* tongues of fire. The Pentecost event was reminiscent of Moses's and the Israelites' charismatic experience of Yahweh at Mt. Sinai (Exod 19–20). Through the Spirit's filling, the disciples gathered in the upper room praised God supernaturally by speaking in foreign tongues. Luke says that outsiders to the event were "amazed and astonished." He writes, "And at this sound the multitude came together, and they were bewildered, because each one was hearing them speak in his own language" (v. 6). Dunn says, *"[Pentecost] was the experience of divine power unexpected in its givenness and in its accompanying features which probably determined the elements of the vision."*[9]

A second charismatic characteristic of the church in Acts is the prevalence of prophecy. After the descent of the Spirit, Peter explains the significance of the unusual events to a perplexed outside crowd. Quoting the prophet Joel, Peter says, "And in the last days it shall be, God declares, that I will pour out my Spirit on all flesh, your sons and your daughters shall prophesy" (2:17). According to Luke, the gift of prophecy is given to "all flesh" as a sign of the new age of the Spirit. The ability to prophesy at

8. Dunn, *Jesus and the Spirit*, 194.

9. Dunn, *Jesus and the Spirit*, 148; emphasis in original.

A POWERFUL PRESENCE

Pentecost was a fulfillment of Moses's hope "that all the LORD's people were prophets and that the LORD would put his Spirit on them!" (Num 11:29). The gift of prophecy ushered God's people into a new era of divine immediacy and power. Dunn observes, "Their consciousness of Spirit was in large part an awareness of inspiration, of direct contact with God."[10] This newfound immediacy with God inspired the church to witness boldly about Jesus and his resurrection (Acts 2:29; 4:13, 29, 31; 28:31). The Spirit of prophecy in Acts is poured out upon all flesh, but some emerged with a greater measure of grace than others. Those who possessed the gift of prophecy with more regularity and frequency were considered "prophets" (11:27; 13:1; 15:32; 21:10).

A third charismatic characteristic of the church in Acts is how Pentecost fueled the church's mission. Dunn says, "[In Acts,] Pentecost provided an indispensable impulse to mission." He adds, "It is the gift of the Spirit which determines and regulates the expansion of the church's mission (see especially 8.14ff.; 10.44ff.; so also 6.10; 8.39; 10.19f.; 13.1ff.; 15.28; 16.6f.; 19.1–7), and it is evident that one of Luke's aims in Acts is to demonstrate that the gift of the Spirit is the crucial factor in conversation and initiation."[11] According to Luke, the church's mission would have no impact without the Spirit. At crucial points in the Acts story, the Holy Spirit leads, directs, and positions the church toward fulfilling its mission.

Finally, a fourth charismatic characteristic is how miraculous gifts of the Spirit propelled the church in its mission. Miraculous gifts were often described in Acts as "signs and wonders" (2:43; 4:30; 5:12; 6:8; 14:3; 15:12). The early church's charismatic demonstrations of signs and wonders were reminiscent of the OT judges and prophets who were moved by the Spirit's power and performed extraordinary deeds. Signs and wonders were not ancillary to the Acts story but central to the church's way of life. Dunn writes, "It is quite clear that Luke intends us to see the early community as living in an

10. Dunn, *Jesus and the Spirit*, 170.
11. Dunn, *Jesus and the Spirit*, 153.

88

BIBLICAL AND EXEGETICAL ANALYSIS: ESCHATOLOGICAL ENTHUSIASM

atmosphere of the miraculous."[12] The prominence of signs and wonders reflects the church's belief that they were living in a new Mosaic age (Exod 7:3). Signs and wonders involved healings (Acts 3:1–10), exorcisms (8:7), miracles of judgment (5:1–11), miraculous escapes by angelic assistance (e.g., Peter and Paul [5:19–24; 12:6–11]), and even a miracle by Peter's shadow (19:11).

These signs and wonders often occur through the practice of the laying on of hands (5:12; 9:12, 17; 14:3; 19:11; 28:8). Dunn says that the laying on of hands is "seen as an action of prophetic symbolism—the hand of the healer representing the hand of the Lord (= God)—the real power behind the healing."[13] The early church moved in signs and wonders because it possessed charismatic *authority*. Dunn writes,

> The principal source of authority was evidently understood to be the *Spirit*. . . . The authority of leadership, of evangelism, of counseling, of teaching, was the charismatic authority of the Spirit (6.3, 5, 10; 7.55; 11.24; 18.25). The Spirit seems to have been regarded as the directing force within the community (5.3, 9; 9.31; cf. 7.51), and was certainly understood as the inspiration and guiding hand in mission (8.29, 39; 10.19; 11.12; 13.2, 4; 16.6f.; 19.21; 20.22).[14]

This charismatic authority was not inherent to any particular individual or community but came simply "in the name of Jesus."

The Charismatic Spirit in Paul's Churches

Dunn explores the charismatic faith of the apostle Paul and his churches. Paul's churches were charismatic communities that shared in the experience of the Spirit or what the apostle calls "the fellowship of the Spirit" (2 Cor 13:14; Phil 2:1). Paul's churches consisted of a charismatic membership where each person could

---

12. Dunn, *Jesus and the Spirit*, 163.

13. Dunn, *Jesus and the Spirit*, 165.

14. Dunn, *Jesus and the Spirit*, 176; emphasis in original.

A POWERFUL PRESENCE

manifest special graces or charismatic gifts from the Spirit to build up the body. Paul sees the church as a unified but diverse charismatic community in Christ.

Dunn argues that Paul's understanding of the Spirit (*pneuma*) is essentially an *experiential* concept. Paul's teaching on *pneuma* is derived mainly from his experience as an apostle. The Spirit who led Paul in starting churches is the same power that operates in a person's *heart*—his or her emotions, will, and thoughts. The Spirit is the power of inner life that makes faith in God essentially *real* (Rom 2:28; 2 Cor 3; Gal 4:6; Phil 3:3; Eph 1:17). The Spirit is also the power of God that transforms people into the image of Christ. Dunn writes,

> The Spirit is that power which transforms a man from the inside out, so that metaphors of cleansing and consecration become matters of actual experience in daily living (1 Cor 6.9–11). The Spirit is the source of that wave of love and upsurge of joy which overwhelms the force that oppose from without (Rom 5.5; 1 Thess 1.5). The Spirit is the power that liberates from a rule-book mentality of casuistry and fear (Rom 8.2, 15; 1 Cor 3.17), so that ethical decisions become a matter of inward convictions and spontaneous love, of walking by the Spirit, rather than unquestioning obedience to a law (Rom 7.6; 2 Cor 3.3; Gal 5.25).[15]

Charisma/Charismata and Pneumatika

Dunn examines two families of Greek words from Paul's writings associated with charismatic experience. *Charisma/charismata* (gift/gifts) and *pneumatika* (spiritual gifts/things) are words that have grace at the root and express the "visible outworkings of divine grace."[16] As expressions of grace, they exist to strengthen the church. Paul understands the charismatic gifts as divine services that manifest God's invisible presence (v. 7). The spiritual

15. Dunn, *Jesus and the Spirit*, 201.
16. Dunn, *Jesus and the Spirit*, 203.

BIBLICAL AND EXEGETICAL ANALYSIS: ESCHATOLOGICAL ENTHUSIASM

gifts also reveal God's power (*dunamis*) and the Spirit's work (*energema*). God manifests his presence through the charismata to bring resurrection life to his people.

CHARISMA/CHARISMATA

Charisma is a distinctively Pauline concept, says Dunn. *Charisma* is "an event, an action enabled by divine power; charisma is divine energy accomplishing a particular result (in word and deed) through the individual."[17] "The word *charisma* overlaps with *charis* in its range of meaning, first, as the gracious act of God in Christ and its effect on human justification (Rom 6:23), and second, as corresponding to particular gifts given to the believer (i.e., Rom 1.11)."[18] Paul's most frequent use of charisma involves manifesting grace within the community of faith. For example, Paul writes in 1 Corinthians, "Now there are varieties of gifts [*charismata*], but the same Spirit" (12:4). Paul says there are "varieties" of charismata, consisting of divine utterances of wisdom, knowledge, ability to distinguish between spirits, and various kinds of tongues. In his Letter to the Romans, Paul mentions other charismata, such as prophecy, service, teaching, exhortation, and giving (Rom 12:6–7).

PNEUMATIKOS

Dunn says Paul uses *pneumatikos* almost as distinctively as *charisma*. He writes, "*Pneumatikos* is Paul's way of saying that something belongs to the Spirit, embodies the Spirit, manifests the Spirit, or is of the essence of the Spirit."[19] Paul uses *pneumatikos* as an adjective to describe something spiritual, as a noun to refer to a spiritual person, and as a plural neuter to mean spiritual things. For example, in 1 Cor 2:13, Paul describes "spiritual people" (*pneumatika*) as those the Spirit influences. In 1 Cor 9:11, Paul contrasts

17. Dunn, *Jesus and the Spirit*, 209.
18. Dunn, *Jesus and the Spirit*, 203.
19. Dunn, *Jesus and the Spirit*, 208.

A POWERFUL PRESENCE

pneumatika with "material things" in describing the spiritual nature of the apostle's ministry.

MIRACLES, HEALINGS, FAITH, AND PROPHECY

In 1 Cor 12, Paul mentions specific manifestations of the Spirit that involve extraordinary phenomena, such as miracles, healings, faith, and prophecy. Paul uses the word *dunameis* to describe miracles, which involve an overt display of divine power. Paul witnessed divine miracles occurring in his churches (Rom 15:19; 2 Cor 12:12; Gal 3:5). Dunn explains, "By *dunameis* Paul is evidently thinking of events in which people (and things?) were visibly and beneficially affected in an extraordinary way by a nonrational power through the medium of Paul and other believers."[20] Instances or gifts of healing(s) were also present in Paul's churches. First Corinthians 12:9 represents a firsthand testimony that healings occurred where Paul preached. Dunn says that the gift of faith here in Paul is not justifying faith but "that mysterious surge of confidence which sometimes arises within a man in a particular situation of need or challenge and which give him an otherly certainty and assurance that God is about to act through a word or through an action (such as laying hands on someone sick)."[21]

The gift of prophecy is crucial to Paul's churches (Rom 12:6; 1 Cor 12:10; 1 Thess 5:20; 1 Tim 1:18; 4:14). Indeed, the apostle prefers prophecy over other Spirit-inspired ministries like tongues (1 Cor 14:1). He exhorts the Corinthians to "earnestly desire the spiritual gifts, especially that you may prophesy" (v. 1). The apostle prefers prophecy to tongues because "the one who prophesies builds up the church"—not just himself (v. 4). Some NT interpreters understand prophecy in Paul as akin to preaching; however, Dunn contends that prophecy involves inspired, revelatory speech, given the frequency with which it is associated with foretelling and forthtelling (1 Cor 14:26–32). Indeed, the author

20. Dunn, *Jesus and the Spirit*, 210.
21. Dunn, *Jesus and the Spirit*, 211.

92

says that prophecy and revelation are near synonyms in Paul. Prophecy is not a matter solely of rational thought but opens the community to a transcendent reality. Due to its revelatory power, prophecy speaks to the *whole* person. Dunn argues that prophecy is the "guarantor of spiritual health and growth [for the church]." He says that without prophecy, "the community cannot exist as the body of Christ; it has been abandoned by God."[22]

Exegesis of Paul's Use of "Power" in 1 and 2 Corinthians

Having explored James Dunn's analysis of the charismatic character of early Christianity, a brief look at Paul's understanding of the Spirit and power (*dunamis*) in 1 and 2 Corinthians will clarify the apostle's understanding of God's dynamic action. Exploring the Corinthian correspondences is fitting in light of the frequency with which the Spirit and power are mentioned. Paul uses "Spirit" and "power" almost interchangeably. And much of the apostle's understanding of the Spirit can be found in Paul's Letters to Corinth. On this point, I believe that the Spirit is the key to understanding 1 and 2 Corinthians.[23] Fee observes that in Paul's letter of 1 Corinthians alone, "there are at least 27 (probably 31) references to the Holy Spirit; 15 of 24 occurrences of the adjective *pneumatikos* (Spiritual); [and] the only occurrence of the adverb 'spiritually' (2:14, where Paul clearly intends 'by means of the Spirit')."[24]

In 1 and 2 Corinthians, the apostle contends with status-seeking believers and outsiders who pride themselves on their exceptional supernatural experiences. The Corinthians boasted of being "people of the Spirit" (*pneumatikos*), and indicative of the Greek culture of the time, they attached high social value to great orators and charismatic leaders. As the apostle to the Corinthians, Paul seeks to correct their worldly perspective, arguing for

22. Dunn, *Jesus and the Spirit*, 233.

23. Gordon Fee makes this point concerning Paul's letter of 1 Corinthians (*God's Empowering Presence*, 83), but I believe it can be extended to 2 Corinthians too.

24. Fee, *God's Empowering Presence*, 82.

A POWERFUL PRESENCE

a true vision of what it means to be a "people of the Spirit." Paul redefines a "Spirit person" by considering the gospel of Christ and his own example as Christ's apostle. The Corinthians were also veering toward a form of Christian triumphalism, where they believed they had already received the fullness of salvation through their participation in the Spirit (1 Cor 4:8). This Christian triumphalism resulted in an over-realized eschatology that denied the necessity of Christ's return and the body's resurrection (15:12–58). In response, Paul writes the occasional letters of 1 and 2 Corinthians to remind the church of their saved but transitory state in the Spirit. The apostle hopes to reorient the church *eschatologically*—toward the ultimate hope of Christ's return and the body's resurrection (1 Cor 13:8–9; 15:12–58).

In 1 Corinthians, Paul defends his message and ministry against self-promoting agitators within the congregation. Certain members of the Corinthian church were critical of Paul's (apparently) unimpressive social credentials and speaking ability. This small yet influential group threatened to divide the church, even steering the congregation away from the apostle and his message (1:10; 4:1). In his defense, Paul does not seek to compare himself with other orators (to gain the Corinthians' patronage) but to point them back to his gospel. The first mention of "power" in 1 Corinthians comes at the end of Paul's opening call for unity (1:17). Paul reminds the church of the gospel he preached and the Corinthians believed. Paul explains that his gospel was of a *crucified* Messiah who died in human weakness. Paul contrasts Christ's weakness with the Corinthians' desire for worldly status and power. Paul declares that the gospel of the crucified Savior demonstrated the power of God, as evidenced through the Corinthians' faith. At the close of his opening section, the apostle points out the irony of the Corinthians' status seeking by reminding them they were not privileged socially when they first believed. Nevertheless, Christ died for them (vv. 18–31).

BIBLICAL AND EXEGETICAL ANALYSIS: ESCHATOLOGICAL ENTHUSIASM

God's Power in Human Weakness (1 Cor 2:3–5)

In 1 Cor 2, Paul highlights his physically weak condition when he first arrived in Corinth and preached to them. Paul parallels his own weakness with Christ's weakness on the cross to underscore the Corinthians' pride and boasting. He writes, "And I, when I came to you, brothers, did not come proclaiming to you the testimony of God with lofty speech or wisdom" (2:1). Rather than relying on "lofty speech and wisdom," the apostle decided to know nothing among them "except Jesus Christ and him crucified" (v. 2). Paul then recounts his physically weak condition when preaching to them. He writes,

> And I was with you in weakness and in fear and much trembling, and my speech and message were not in plausible words of wisdom, but in demonstration of the Spirit and of power, so that your faith might not rest in the wisdom of men but in the power of God. (1 Cor 2:3–5)

In describing himself as coming in "weakness and fear and much trembling," Paul juxtaposes his physically weak condition with the Spirit's power. Paul's weakness highlights the Spirit's power. The apostle explains that God allowed Paul to preach in a physically weak state "so that your faith might not rest in the wisdom of men but in the power of God" (v. 5).

Paul's point in this passage is clear: the Corinthians' faith demonstrates God's power in human weakness.[25] Paul's physically weak condition (i.e., "fear and much trembling") led to a transparent viewing of the Holy Spirit and his power. The apostle's weakness only heightened God's power amid the Corinthians' faith. In sum, in only the first two chapters of 1 Corinthians, Paul underscores how God's power is demonstrated in human weakness. God's power is demonstrated in the weakness of the crucified Messiah, in the low rank of the Corinthian believers, and in Paul's own physically weak condition.

---

25. Paul makes a similar argument again in 1 Cor 4:9–13.

A POWERFUL PRESENCE

God's Power in the Spiritual Gifts (1 Cor 12:7–11)

The passage of 1 Cor 12:7–11 is part of the largest section of Spirit material in the Pauline corpus.[26] In four verses the Spirit is mentioned six times (vv. 7–11). In this passage, Paul addresses issues concerning corporate worship, as he argues for a diversity of charismatic gifts at the church. Corinthian worship had become dominated by the practice of speaking in tongues. The Corinthians were enamored with the gift of tongues because, as those who prided themselves as "people of the Spirit" (*pneumatikois*), tongues enabled them to speak in a heavenly or angelic-like manner (13:1). Paul does not invalidate the gift of tongues, but he redirects the church toward a healthy practice of the spiritual gifts. The apostle encourages the Corinthians to exercise a variety of gifts and for the gifts to be administered in a way that leads to mutual edification rather than spiritual showmanship.

After laying out his criteria for determining what is and is not Spirit-inspired speech (12:3), Paul grounds his instruction in God's triune nature (vv. 4–6). In defining what it means to "speak in the Spirit," he provides insight into how the Spirit is "manifested" in the church. Despite the contemporary use of this passage as a systematic treatment of the spiritual gifts, Paul's emphasis here is on the Spirit's "manifestations." He writes,

> [7] To each is given the manifestation of the Spirit for the common good. [8] For to one is given through the Spirit the utterance of wisdom, and to another the utterance of knowledge according to the same Spirit, [9] to another faith by the same Spirit, to another gifts of healing by the one Spirit, [10] to another the working of miracles, to another prophecy, to another the ability to distinguish between spirits, to another various kinds of tongues, to another the interpretation of tongues. [11] All these are empowered by one and the same Spirit, who apportions to each one individually as he wills.

26. Fee, *God's Empowering Presence*, 146.

Verse 7 serves as Paul's thesis of the passage. Paul highlights the diversity of the charismata ("to each one"), stating that the gifts are a "manifestation of the Spirit." The Greek word here, "manifestation" (*phanerosis*), is rare. It means to publicly announce or exhibit (see also 2 Cor 4:2).[27] In other words, God publicly announces or exhibits his Spirit activity in and through the spiritual gifts. As manifestations *of the Spirit*, they reveal God's emanating power. In emphasizing that the gifts are *from the Spirit*, Paul is saying that they do not come from any particular "spiritual" person.

After stating his thesis, Paul grounds his exhortation on the diversity of the Spirit's manifestations using several illustrations (vv. 8–10). Paul lists nine different charismata that reflect the breath of the Spirit's activity. The manifestations cited here are a representative, not exhaustive, list. Paul's emphasis lies in the *supernatural* action of the Spirit, for all the gifts listed are visible. (Paul addresses the more mundane gifts of the body later in the passage [vv. 28–30].)

The first two manifestations mentioned are verbal utterances involving wisdom (*sophia*) and knowledge (*gnosis*) (v. 8). Paul first addresses wisdom and knowledge due to the Corinthians' fascination with worldly forms of wisdom and knowledge, attested to earlier in the letter (1:17—2:16; 8:1–3, 7). Paul seeks to redefine Spirit-inspired wisdom and knowledge considering the cross of Christ. Paul argues that wisdom and knowledge become Spirit-*ual* (*pneumatikois*) when exercised in love and humility, leading to mutual edification.

Next, Paul mentions gifts of faith, healing, miracles, prophecy, and distinguishing between spirits (vv. 9–10b). Regarding faith, even though in other letters Paul describes it as a grace that leads to salvation in Christ (Rom 6:23; 1 Cor 11:29), here he means the gift of faith large enough to "remove mountains" (1 Cor 13:2). Fee describes this kind of faith as the "supernatural conviction that God will reveal his power or mercy in a special way in a special instance."[28] Considering gifts of healing, Paul mentions their

27. Thiselton, *First Epistle to Corinthians*, 936.

28. Fee, *First Epistle to Corinthians*, 658.

occurrence in this passage and then again in vv. 28 and 30. Despite modern skepticism toward divine healing, they were common in Paul's churches (2 Cor 12:12; Rom 15:19). For divine healing, Paul and other NT writers draw upon the prophetic tradition where divine healing was understood to accompany the new messianic age (Isa 53:4). Manifestations of miracles could involve healings and other supernatural actions of the Spirit that defy natural explanation. Fee observes that the Greek word for "miracles" is the ordinary word for "power," as it was associated with the Spirit of God in Jewish antiquity.[29] Paul's understanding of prophecy was thoroughly conditioned by his history in Judaism. Fee writes, "[Prophecy] consisted of spontaneous, Spirit-inspired, intelligible messages, orally delivered in the gathering assembly, intended for the edification or encouragement of the people."[30] Prophets spoke to God's people under the inspiration of the Spirit.

Paul closes his list of Spirit manifestations with the gifts of tongues and the interpretation of tongues. The apostle concludes with tongues not because it is the least gift but because of its misuse in the Corinthians' worship. Paul prefers prophecy to tongues (at least uninterpreted tongues) due to prophecy's edifying and revelatory power. Paul generally favors intelligible speech over unintelligible speech in his congregations (1 Cor 14:19).

In v. 11, Paul concludes his section on the diversity of the Spirit's manifestations by restating his thesis (v. 7). The apostle contends that the Spirit determines the gifts, not the individual. (Although in 12:31 and 14:1, he encourages the church to pursue the gifts.) He reiterates that the various gifts are all "empowered" (*energeo*) by the "one and the same Spirit." Rather than practicing tongues alone, Paul exhorts the Corinthians to allow the Spirit to manifest his manifold gifts (i.e., "to each one").

---

29. Fee, *First Epistle to Corinthians*, 659.

30. Fee, *First Epistle to Corinthians*, 660.

BIBLICAL AND EXEGETICAL ANALYSIS: ESCHATOLOGICAL ENTHUSIASM

God's Grace in Human Weakness (2 Cor 12:9–10)

Like his letter of 1 Corinthians, in 2 Corinthians Paul addresses a charismatic church that continues to wrestle with the apostle's message and authority. However, unlike in 1 Corinthians, where his challengers come from within the church, 2 Corinthians involves insurgents outside the Corinthian congregation. In this highly polemical letter, Paul minces no words regarding his detractors. He says they "peddle God's word" (2:17); require unnecessary "letters of recommendation," which only serve themselves (3:1); and "practice cunning or tamper with God's word" (4:2). Although the insurgents consider themselves "super apostles," Paul sees them as "false apostles, deceitful workmen, disguising themselves as apostles of Christ" (11:13). Their influence was dangerously leading the Corinthians toward "another Jesus," "another spirit," and "a different gospel" altogether (11:4). Fee suggests these outsiders were "Jewish Christians who were contending for a form of 'Jewishness' in the Corinthians' understanding of Christ and the Spirit."[31]

In 2 Cor 12:1–12, Paul indulges in a "fool's boast" to counteract the agitators' prideful posturing. Paul matches—even exceeds—their foolish boasts point for point. Paul turns their boasts of extraordinary spiritual experiences on their heads, even parodying them, by recounting his own extraordinary "visions and revelations." The apostle does so, however, reluctantly, understanding that nothing is to be gained from such boasting (v. 1). Paul shares one particular dramatic spiritual encounter where he was taken up into "paradise" or what he calls "the third heaven." During this extraordinary spiritual experience, Paul "heard inexpressible things, things that no one is permitted to tell" (v. 4). Despite the surpassingly great revelation he received, however, Paul was given a "thorn in his flesh." Paul does not identify the "thorn" but only names its source—"a messenger of Satan" (v. 7). He explains the thorn was given to keep him from boasting and becoming conceited because of the surpassingly great revelations he has received. Paul relays

---

31. Fee, *God's Empowering Presence*, 284.

A POWERFUL PRESENCE

that he asked God three times to remove the thorn, but each time the Lord demurred. He writes,

> 9 But he said to me, "My grace is sufficient for you, for my power is made perfect in weakness." Therefore I will boast all the more gladly of my weaknesses, so that the power of Christ may rest upon me. 10 For the sake of Christ, then, I am content with weaknesses, insults, hardships, persecutions, and calamities. For when I am weak, then I am strong.

Paul explains that God reminded him of the presence of his grace (*charis*) in his life despite the thorn. God's grace—his generous goodness in Paul's life—is enough to sustain the apostle and to help him persevere with the thorn. The Lord explains, "For my power is made perfect in weakness." God says his otherworldly power is perfected in the apostle's weakness. The two English words "made perfect" are one Greek word (*teleioo*), which means to bring to an end by completion, reach a goal, or finish.[32] God reminds Paul that his divine *dunamis* is perfected not only in ecstasy but also in the apostle's frailty. Through this divine revelation, Paul has learned to be "content with weakness, insults, hardships, persecution, and calamities," concluding, "when I am weak, then I am strong" (v. 10).

First Corinthians 12:9–10 is an instance when supernatural intervention does not occur, despite the earnest prayer of an apostle. Instead of deliverance, Paul receives a thorn and is supplied with divine grace, which is much better.[33] Paul's example demonstrates that even "people of the Spirit" must endure life's difficulties, sometimes without supernatural intervention. Nonetheless, God's grace is powerfully present and sufficient. Divine grace enables Paul to persevere in faith and endure the thorn in his flesh. Divine grace is enough for Paul because God's power is manifested not only in supernatural experiences but also in human weakness. God's power is perfected even in weakness. Therefore, Paul

32. Vine et al., *Vine's Expository Dictionary*, s.v. "Perfect."

33. Jesus also offered up a threefold prayer to God in the garden of Gethsemane, which was refused (Mark 14:33–41).

BIBLICAL AND EXEGETICAL ANALYSIS: ESCHATOLOGICAL ENTHUSIASM

embraces "weakness, insults, hardships, persecutions, and calamities," knowing that these, too, bring him closer to God. Paul's account of his thorn shifts the Corinthians' focus away from ecstasy toward Christ and his grace. Through grace, human frailty and weakness become the terrain of God's supernatural power. God demonstrates his divine power in the weakness of his Spirit people, just as he did through Christ and his cross.

In his Letter to the Romans, Paul says something similar about the divine power and grace considering the Spirit. He writes, "Likewise, the Spirit helps us in our weakness. For we do not know what to pray for as we ought, but the Spirit himself intercedes for us with groanings too deep for words" (Rom 8:26). The Spirit "helps us in our weakness" through companionship, intercession, and testifying to us that we are God's children (8:16). In this way, the apostle understood God's power is demonstrated in various ways. God's power is demonstrated, for example, in the weakness of his preaching (1 Cor 2:3–5), in the charismatic gifts (1 Cor 12:7–11), in the presence of a thorn in his flesh (2 Cor 12:9–10), and in the groans of a sojourner in distress (Rom 8:26). God's power is most visibly demonstrated in the weakness of a crucified Messiah.

In this way, Paul understands God's power *eschatologically*. The apostle declares that God's power has broken into the world but only as a "deposit," not a consummation (2 Cor 1:22). The Holy Spirit is present in the church as the "firstfruits" of the glory to be revealed (Rom 8:23). Paul assures the Corinthians that they have not "arrived" spiritually and that more is to come when Christ returns. In the meantime, God's Spirit people participate in his kingdom *partially*, like looking into a mirror dimly (1 Cor 13:12). In examining the Holy Spirit and power in Paul's writings, Gordon Fee underscores their eschatological dimensions. He writes, "On the one hand, the future had broken in so powerfully that signs and wonders and miracles are simply matter-of-fact (1 Cor 12:8–12; Gal 3:5); on the other hand, the Spirit also empowers for endurance in the midst of adversity (Col 1:11; 2 Cor 12:9–10)—and for

A POWERFUL PRESENCE

everything else as we endure, awaiting the final glory, of which the Spirit is the guarantee."[34]

Excursus: Divine Healing in Paul

A study of 2 Cor 12:8–12 focusing on "Paul's thorn" often leads readers of the NT to questions concerning Christian expectation of divine healing. Conservative Evangelicals frequently point to the passage of Paul's thorn as an example of when divine healing is *not* "God's will." In these instances, traditional Evangelicals stress the importance of perseverance in the face of sickness. Christians may pray for healing, they say, but not necessarily *expect* it. Charismatic Christians for their part tend to emphasize God's desire to heal sickness. Bethel Church takes a stronger position than most, asserting it is *always* God's will to heal, with only a few exceptions. As mentioned, Bethel referred to the Gospels, where Jesus healed everyone who asked him, to support their position (Matt 15:30). Bethel leaders also cited passages like Ps 103:3 ("who forgives all your sins and heals all your diseases") and Isa 53:5 ("and by his stripes we are healed"), to assert that physical healing is a part of Christ's redemption on the cross and therefore a present expectation in this life through faith. Additionally, they argued from passages like 1 Tim 2:4 or 2 Pet 3:9, contending that just as God "desires all people to be saved and to come to the knowledge of the truth" (although not all are saved), God also desires all to be healed (although not all are healed).

When physical healing does not occur, Bethel leaders sometimes explain its absence as the result of interference of dark spirits or the need to persevere in faith and prayer, like Jesus's parable of the persistent widow (Luke 18:1–8). Bethel sees spiritual and human factors at play in healing, despite it being "God's will." They draw biblical precedent from examples such as when the angel Michael was prevented from helping Daniel due to a spiritual battle (Dan 10:13). They observe that even Jesus was limited

---

34. Fee, *God's Empowering Presence*, 8.

BIBLICAL AND EXEGETICAL ANALYSIS: ESCHATOLOGICAL ENTHUSIASM

in healing others in his hometown due to their lack of faith (Matt 15:38). Generally speaking, charismatics view the world as a free and open space where cosmic spiritual battles occur between good and evil forces, with God standing sovereign over it all (Ps. 82; Eph 6:10–18).

Observations Concerning Divine Healing

A few observations will shed light on Christian expectations of healing as evidenced in Paul. First, Paul distinguishes between sickness and suffering in his writings. Readers of the NT often conflate sickness and suffering, but Paul sees them differently. Sickness is viewed negatively by Paul, while suffering is sometimes understood positively. Sickness involves bodily, physical dis-*ease*, while suffering involves persecution from others. Paul uses the NT Greek word *pascho* to describe suffering but never regarding physical sickness (Rom 8:18; 2 Cor 1:5; Phil 3:10; Col 1:24; 2 Tim 3:11). Most importantly, Paul (and other NT writers) *never see value or virtue in sickness.* While suffering is sometimes viewed positively by the apostle, sickness is not. Sickness is the result of sin, the fall, or demonic activity and is always against the will of God (1 Thess 5:23; 3 John 1:2). God intends to heal physical sickness either in this life or the next.

However, Paul sees positive qualities associated with persecution and suffering (2 Cor 1:5–7; Col 1:24; 2 Tim 2:3). For example, the apostle considers suffering virtuous when writing to the Philippian church, stating, "I want to know Christ in the power of his resurrection and the fellowship of sharing in his suffering" (Phil 3:10). But with sickness, Paul (and other NT writers) always desire the sick to be healed (Phil 2:25–27; Jas 5:14). The only occasion when Paul mentions any sanctifying properties associated with sickness is *negatively*, that is, to correct bad behavior. For example, Paul says that some of the Corinthians became weak, sick, and even died because they engaged in the Lord's Supper in an unworthy manner. In this case, it was not "God's will" for the Corinthians to engage in the Lord's Supper in an unholy manner, but because of their ungodly

103

A POWERFUL PRESENCE

behavior, they brought judgment upon themselves (1 Cor 11:30). It seems clear that Paul and other NT writers encouraged their followers to endure suffering but to pray for the sick to be healed, for sickness contradicts the will of God.

Finally, the apostle understands divine healing *eschatologically*. In writing to his churches Paul understands that divine healing can be partial, provisional, and ambiguous.[35] This is an important point. Because the church lives between the time of the kingdom's inauguration and consummation, Paul understands that divine healing will not always result in permanent lifelong health. In his writings, Paul and his companions sometimes became sick or ill, and these ailments disrupted their fellowship and mission to preach the gospel. However, even in these instances, Paul recognizes God's sovereignty. For example, Paul reminds the church in Galatia that he stayed with them due to an illness, which led to his preaching the gospel there (Gal 4:13). Also, Paul encouraged Timothy to add wine to his water to treat his chronic stomach ailment (1 Tim 5:23). Paul left Trophimus, another ministry partner, in Miletus so that Trophimus could recover from illness (2 Tim 4:20). And finally, Paul's faithful friend and fellow church planter, Ephaphroditus, almost died because of sickness. Yet Paul affirms God's goodness in his healing, stating, "But God had mercy on him, and not only on him but on me also, lest I should have sorrow upon sorrow" (Phil 2:27).

In addition to acknowledging the presence of sickness among believers, Paul also recognizes the *mortal* condition of the body. Paul understands that followers of Christ may die before Christ's return, and the apostle is not surprised by it. The Thessalonian congregation was unsettled by the passing of some of their members, so Paul comforts them of the future hope of resurrection (1 Thess 4:13–18). Although we do not know the cause of death of these Thessalonian believers, it would be not be surprising if some had died from sickness, not just natural causes. Paul understood that even the great OT prophet, Elisha, died due to

35. I received this insight from Ken Blue and his very helpful book *Authority to Heal*.

an illness (2 Kgs 13:14). Because Paul sees the Spirit and salvation eschatologically, he understands that sickness, disease, and death will be eradicated only when Christ returns. In the moment of Christ's return, the dead in Christ will rise first, and those still alive will be taken up in eternal life with renewed bodies (Rom 8:11; 1 Cor 15:42–44, 51–52; 1 Thess 4:15–18).

Returning again to "Paul's thorn" (2 Cor 12:1–12), many conservative (and nonconservative) Christians point to it as an example of when it is God's will *not* to heal. Even though Paul does not explicitly identify his thorn, some Christians see in his description the location of his troubles, that is, "*in the flesh.*" They argue that since Paul describes his thorn as "in the flesh," it must have been a physical ailment of some kind.

There are a few problems with this view, however. First, as stated previously, nowhere in 2 Cor 12 does Paul describe his thorn as a *physical* problem. Paul is apt to mention physical sickness elsewhere in his letters, but he does not mention it here. Second, and as charismatic Christians are quick to point out, the phrase "thorn in the flesh" is used elsewhere in Scripture; both occur in the OT. In each instance, "thorn in the flesh" describes Israel's enemies (Num 33:55; Josh 23:13). It seems that God left some of Israel's enemies in the promised land to test his people. When understood this way, "thorn in the flesh" works like the common idiom "a pain in the neck." When something is "a pain in the neck," English speakers typically do not mean a physical ailment but that something or someone who is causing them distress. This observation leads us to the third and strongest argument against understanding Paul's thorn as a physical ailment, which is the passage's context. In 2 Cor 12:1–12, Paul is addressing problems caused by outsiders to the Corinthian church. These insurgents questioned Paul's gospel and authority, leading the Corinthians toward "a different gospel." Considering this context, the apostle's mention of "a thorn in the flesh" suggests that he is referring to the problems caused by the outside insurgents. Therefore, I argue, along with Craig Keener,

A POWERFUL PRESENCE

that the most probable understanding of Paul's "thorn" is a group of outsiders disrupting the church and the apostle.[36]

Conclusion

In conclusion, whether one sees physical healing as sometimes or always "God's will" or "God's desire," divine healing is a present reality in the Spirit.[37] Jesus continues his messianic healing ministry today through the church in the power of the Spirit. It is a ministry of love to a broken world. However, the church's healing ministry will always be partial, provisional, or ambiguous until Christ returns. The church is anointed by the Spirit, but not in fullness (John 3:34). Embracing this eschatological reality and tension shapes the church's expectation regarding healing. Nonetheless, the Spirit of God helps us in our weakness. The Spirit intercedes for the church with groans and longings too deep for words. Along with the Spirit and all of creation, the church eagerly awaits our final adoption as sons and daughters, the redemption of our bodies (Rom 8:23). This is our Christian hope and expectation, and as Paul says, "It is in this hope we are saved" (v. 24).

Bethel Church's Charismatic Christianity

Considering Dunn's analysis of early Christianity and the exegesis of Paul's use of power in 1 and 2 Corinthians, Bethel Church embodies the charismatic character of early Christianity. Regarding the early Christians, Dunn says, "Their gospel was in large measure the expression of their experience."[38] Dunn explains that the early churches were charismatic communities that participated in

36. Craig Keener reaches the same conclusion regarding the identity of Paul's thorn (*1–2 Corinthians*, 240).

37. Millard Erickson makes a helpful distinction between God's wish and God's will. He writes, "The former is God's general intention, the values with which he is pleased. The latter is God's specific intention in a given situation, what he decides shall actually occur" (*Introducing Christian Doctrine*, 117).

38. Dunn, *Jesus and the Spirit*, 13.

106

BIBLICAL AND EXEGETICAL ANALYSIS: ESCHATOLOGICAL ENTHUSIASM

the shared experience of the Spirit and consisted of a charismatic membership that manifested extraordinary graces, or charismatic gifts. The purpose of these Spirit manifestations was to build up the body of Christ. Bethel's worship, community life, and ministry are shaped by their experience of the Spirit as anchored in Christ through their reading and retelling of Scripture.

Bethel reflects the charismatic character of the early church in three ways. First, Bethel believes they are anointed with the same Spirit that anointed Jesus during his baptism, as shown in the Gospels. This Spirit anointing empowers Bethel toward supernatural ministry. Just as Jesus was a miracle worker anointed with divine authority, Bethel expects signs, wonders, and miracles to occur in and through their community. Indeed, Bethel members heal the sick, deliver the demonized, and perform mighty deeds. Bethel's supernatural "anointing" draws people like Rebecca Cupp and Kevin to leave their homes to move to Redding, California. When my friend from England arrived, she visited Bethel's healing rooms. She received healing prayer for her decades-long tinnitus and was miraculously healed. The same dynamic power at work in Jesus's ministry was manifested in her life. For Bethel, Jesus is the standard of ministry. Bethel seeks to follow Jesus in faith, ethics, and supernatural power, not in ethics alone. Although the Gospels never portray Jesus as experiencing ecstatic expressions, Bethel looks to continue Jesus's ministry of "signs, wonders, and miracles" in the modern world.

Also consistent with Dunn, Bethel is an enthusiastic and charismatic community like the early church in Acts. Bethel reflects the nascent church in Acts in four ways. First, the event of Pentecost is central to Bethel's life and imagination. Pentecost shapes Bethel's worship, enthusiasm, ministry, and vision for mission. The Spirit's baptism that occurred at Pentecost serves as Bethel's paradigm for spirituality. Bethel does not look to grow ministry programs or attract seekers but focuses on charismatic encounters with God through the Holy Spirit. Like Pentecost, Bethel understands their enthusiasm will attract interest as well as ridicule. Nonetheless, Bethel continues to seek God in mighty power through the Spirit's

A POWERFUL PRESENCE

unusual manifestations. Second, the gift of prophecy is central to Bethel's ministry. BSSM students are trained to share prophetic words with believers and unbelievers alike. Bethel often invites outside "prophets" to speak to BSSM students, at conferences, and with Bethel's general community. BSSM revival group pastors frequently operate as prophets, perhaps even more than as "pastors" or "teachers." Bethel speaks of establishing "a prophetic culture" where everyone in the church can administer inspired words. One can receive a prophetic word at Bethel during worship services, at revival groups, or even in the bathroom. Third, consistent with Dunn's analysis of the church in Acts, the Holy Spirit is central to Bethel's community life and ministry. Great attention is given to the person and power of the Holy Spirit, as evidenced in their preaching, teaching, and ministry training. Fourth, like in Acts, Bethel looks to supernatural gifts to empower its members for mission. Bethel members are sent out to proclaim the gospel armed with extraordinary gifts, like faith, healing, miracles, prophecy, and words of knowledge. For example, David, a BSSM second-year student, opened the door to the gospel through a "word of knowledge" to a stranger. The word of knowledge resonated with the man, leading him to receive Christ in the frozen food section of the grocery store. These supernatural gifts opened new pathways for the gospel to emerge in mission. In this way, Bethel follows the early church in Acts, a community empowered by the Spirit gifts to fulfill Christ's missional mandate.

Bethel's charismatic faith is also consistent with Dunn's analysis of the enthusiastic nature of Paul's churches. Dunn argues that Paul viewed the Spirit (*pneuma*) as an *experiential* concept. To Bethel's critics, the megachurch is overly focused on "experiences" or enthusiasm. To Bethel members, they are following in the way of Pauline churches who participated in the "fellowship of the Spirit" (2 Cor 13:14; Phil 2:1). Bethel is not content with routine Sunday services or formal ministry groups; instead, they look to the Spirit's direction, spontaneity, and power in worship, ministry, and community life.

Only the Power Gifts?

However, despite these correspondences with Dunn and the exegetical analysis of 1 and 2 Corinthians, there are two places where Bethel's faith and practice diverges from the analysis above. First, Bethel's practice of spiritual gifts do not reflect the diversity of the Spirit's gifts emphasized by Paul. Bethel's focus is almost exclusively on the "miraculous gifts" of faith, healings, miracles, prophecy, and words of knowledge (1 Cor 12:9–10), leaving minimal space for the "less spectacular" gifts. The heavy focus on the miraculous gifts is demonstrated by the personal testimonies shared at the church, which often involve stories of healing or miracles. BSSM in particular focuses heavily on the miraculous gifts. Perhaps this emphasis is due to being a *supernatural* ministry school. Nonetheless, the heightened attention given to the miraculous comes at times to the neglect of the more mundane gifts and, more importantly, *to the people who operate in them.* For example, John, a BSSM student, shared how those who operated in the power gifts received more attention and praise from Bethel leadership. John (and other BSSM students) referred pejoratively to those who received increased attention as "shiny people." The "less shiny" people did not demonstrate ecstatic expressions or operate prominently in the miraculous gifts.

As a result of the focus on the power gifts, the "less shiny" people at Bethel often feel out of "favor." Indeed, "finding favor" is a social status sought after by BSSM students. Further, Bethel's focus on the power gifts overshadows attention on the Spirit's fruits (Gal 5:22–23). As the exegetical analysis showed, Paul elevated love even above his preferred ministry of prophecy. Paul reminds the Corinthians, "And if I have prophetic powers, and understand all mysteries . . . but have not love, I gain nothing" (1 Cor 13:2–3). Love was more important to Paul than supernatural power or ecstatic manifestations (1 Cor 13:13). Even though I found Bethel to be a loving community, Bethel's favor toward the power gifts leaves some people feeling left out.

A POWERFUL PRESENCE

Flat Eschatology

The other place where Bethel's life and practice do not comport with Dunn and the above exegetical analysis concerns what I would label their "flat eschatology." As Dunn argues, the early church was enthusiastic *and apocalyptic* in character within first-century Judaism. Dunn described the early church as practicing *eschatological enthusiasm.* The Spirit's arrival following Jesus's ascension was a sign that the church was living in the last days. Paul was a "man of the Spirit" par excellence, but he also understood that the Spirit's presence was only the "firstfruits" of what was to come. Paul viewed the Spirit as a "deposit" of the kingdom, not its fulfillment (2 Cor 1:22). In short, Paul understood the church *eschatologically.* The apostle saw the church as living between the time of the kingdom's inauguration and consummation. As such, the church's experience of God's kingdom is *partial.* Christ's kingdom is here "already" but also "not yet." Bethel emphasizes the "already" or "realized" aspects of the kingdom but overlooks its "not yet" dimensions. By highlighting the "already," Bethel collapses the kingdom's future into the present.

Some could characterize Bethel's eschatology as "over realized," but in speaking and listening to Bethel leaders and members, the church seems to suffer more from an "underdeveloped" or "flat" eschatology. Bethel's eschatology is often one dimensional, embracing the Spirit's arrival but conflating it with Jesus's return. Bethel *believes* in Christ's return, as a stated doctrine, but it is rarely mentioned. More importantly, Jesus's return has little influence on Bethel's praxis and imagination. Therefore, Bethel's faith and practice lack an eschatological horizon, as the Spirit's arrival replaces the need for Christ's return.

Bethel's flat eschatology is reflected in, for example, its ministry of healing prayer. Bethel leaders (rightly) pray for and expect divine healing to occur. However, their explanations for when healing does not occur lack eschatological foresight. Bethel understands unrealized healing only as a "divine mystery." As such, Bethel recognizes the kingdom's ambiguous nature but does

BIBLICAL AND EXEGETICAL ANALYSIS: ESCHATOLOGICAL ENTHUSIASM

not acknowledge its partial or provisional dimensions. Bethel's desire to become a "perfect-health zone" reflects this "flat" view. At times, Bethel's eschatology even overshadows the mortality of the human body, something Paul readily acknowledged. For example, one Bethel leader taught that he expected healing to occur for someone ninety-five years old and near death, explaining, "If I don't expect God to heal her, then I'm saying that I want death to be her Savior and not Jesus." To Bethel's credit, they do not fault the person receiving (or giving) healing prayer when healing does not occur. Nonetheless, this Bethel leader's understanding of divine healing overlooked the mortal condition of the body and God's intention to heal it when Christ returns (1 Cor 15:42–54; 1 Thess 4:16). Only when Jesus returns will the sting of death be finally eradicated and our bodies resurrected.

Bethel would do well to embrace a fully orbed eschatology. A fully orbed eschatology recognizes the church lives in time and space, between history and eternity, and within the kingdom's inauguration and consummation. The life of faith in Christ is lived within a tension between power and suffering, the earthly and heavenly, and the mortal and eternal. Through a robust eschatology, Bethel could, on the one hand, embrace divine healing by faith but, on the other hand, find grace and the Spirit's comfort when healing does not occur. Paul recognized the Spirit's power and grace even in unrealized prayer (2 Cor 12:9–10). Moreover, in the anonymous book of Hebrews, the author encourages the church to follow in the faith of the saints of the past who "did not receive what was promised" (11:39). This way, Bethel could find vibrant spiritual life amid the tension between the "already" and "not yet." The apostle Paul recognized that nothing could separate him from the love of God that is in Christ Jesus. He understood that "in all these things we are more than conquerors through him who loved us" (Rom 8:37).

Chapter 6

Proposals for the Future:
The Pentecostal Angel

Authority in spiritual leadership derives from a life in the Spirit, from the minister's personal encounter and ongoing relationship with God.—Dallas Willard, *Hearing God*

IN HIS BOOK *THE Household of God*, missiologist Lesslie Newbigin contends that modern Christianity needs to be criticized and supplemented by what he calls "the Pentecostal angel."[1] Newbigin argues that Western Christianity has conceded too much to the reductions of modernity and therefore has lost the divine unction by which it was first called and commissioned. As a result of its modern concessions, the church lives in a state of anemia. In this anemic state, the church lacks the divine life and energies by which it grows and flourishes. The eternal life Jesus provides for his church involves the ability to see God and act within the realm of the Spirit (John 3:3).[2] Many churches obscure the Spirit's presence and power through various beliefs and practices, so divine life eludes them. By "the Pentecostal angel," Newbigin means "the

---

1. Newbigin, *Household of God*, 121.
2. I draw this definition of spiritual life from Willard, *Hearing God*, 148.

experienced power and presence of the Holy Spirit."[3] He writes, "[Pentecostals] have a strong conviction that new life in the Spirit is an actual experience and received reality, something involving an ontological change in the believer."[4] Newbigin believes that the Holy Spirit's presence and power are the key to the church's future. Through the Spirit, God's people are infused with ever-replenishing vision, vigor, and vitality.

In this score, Bethel Church is a beacon of hope for the twenty-first century. Bethel Church lives and embodies "the experienced power and presence of the Holy Spirit" of which Newbigin speaks. Bethel's experience of the Holy Spirit is one of the main reasons it thrives despite the decline of many churches and historic denominations. Bethel is characterized by its attention to the Holy Spirit, use of spiritual gifts, and direct and evidential experiences with God. As this ethnography has shown, Bethel teems with life and vitality.[5] People travel worldwide to attend a congregation located in Redding, California. Long lines of worshippers form outside the sanctuary doors as people wait for weekend services to start. Some worship services can last up to three or four hours as parishioners seek the manifest presence of Christ. Inside the church, men, women, boys, and girls sing passionately and dance enthusiastically to express their affection for God and joy in the Holy Spirit. Bethel's services and ministries are not curated to attract potential members, grow church membership, or increase the church's political relevance. Their services facilitate unmediated encounters with God. As mentioned, the Holy Spirit is a non-reductive reality at Bethel. Bethel does not rely on big-budget programs or elaborate ministry schemes to further its mission. Bethel focuses on God's presence and looks to the

3. Willard, *Hearing God*, 112.

4. Willard, *Hearing God*, 113.

5. James Stewart also provides a helpful definition of vibrant spiritual life. He writes, "Everything that Paul associates with salvation—joy, and peace, and power, and progress, and moral victory—is gathered up in the one word he uses so constantly, 'life'" (*Man in Christ*, 192–93). Stewart observes that this newness of life in Christ has a supernatural quality to it. This "supernatural quality" is what many of today's churches are missing.

Spirit's referent power to confirm Christ's activity. Bethel reflects a modern-day renewal movement, as they direct their revival fires toward building a burgeoning music ministry, the healing rooms ministry, a new global campus, and various avenues of outreach. Certainly Bethel has its instances of imbalance or excess. Also, Bethel's enthusiastic spirit and ecstatic environment are not for everyone's tastes, nor should they be. However, Bethel offers a picture of vibrant Christianity within late modernity.

Five Proposals for the Future

In this chapter, I offer theological responses and suggestions for the church in late modernity, considering the ethnographic, cultural, and theological analysis above. Here I present five proposals to sharpen the church's vision for the future. The first four proposals regard traditional evangelical churches, considering their cultural and theological hopes. The fifth proposal concerns Bethel Church and, indirectly, neo-charismatic churches like it. With an eye toward practical application, each proposal presents an example of what Alan Roxburgh calls Spirit-led experiments.[6] Spirit-led experiments encourage congregations to discern the work of God in their context. Spirit-led experiments are a part of an iterative process consisting of reflection, experimentation, and evaluation. The Spirit-led experiments presented here serve to stimulate churches to do their own cultural, theological, and spiritual reflection. My underlying conviction in presenting these proposals is that a glorious and unprecedented future awaits the church in America in the twenty-first century. As one author has stated, God is working to bring his new future into being.[7] Through faith, prayer, and courageous leadership—under the direction of the Holy Spirit—the people of God can creatively collaborate with Christ to bring this new future into being.

---

6. Roxburgh, "Missional Leadership Seminar," Northern Seminary, Lisle, IL, Sept. 14–19, 2020.

7. I borrowed this idea from Sine, *Mustard Seed Conspiracy*, 20.

PROPOSALS FOR THE FUTURE: THE PENTECOSTAL ANGEL

1. Focus on God's Presence

The first proposal is a reorientation of the church. This reorientation involves congregations moving away from the strategies of accumulating resources or social relevance to focusing on God's presence. The modern church needs life—vibrant spiritual life. Dynamic spiritual life occurs in the Spirit of God moving in our midst. The Spirit is the breath of life, the Holy One who sanctifies and renews all of creation. As churches attend to the presence of the Christ in their midst through the Spirit, they experience the new life and vitality that only God brings (John 7:38).

For churches to move from the strategies of resources and relevance, church leaders must reimagine the church's identity and call considering the Spirit. The church is not a vendor of religious goods and services but the people of God's *presence*. As the people of God, the church moves from energy expenditure to rest (Heb 4:3), from having-mode to being-mode, and from marketing strategies to the person and work of the Spirit (John 15:15; Rom 8:15). The church is the temple of the Holy Spirit, not "a spiritual resource center." Delighting in God's presence is the chief end of humankind, and as John Calvin observes, the *fons vitae* (well of life).[8] Terry Cross explains that the "people of God's presence" rely "heavily on the Spirit's work in individuals and in the community."[9] Through the Spirit, the people of God experience him *directly*. Through direct encounters, the people of God encounter Christ, Spirit to spirit (Rom 8:16). Also, the circle of divine presence is the circle of otherworldly power (v. 11). God's Spirit manifests resurrected power to save sinners, heal the sick, deliver the oppressed, and set captives free.

A Spirit-led experiment for churches is to create extended worship and ministry sessions for people to enjoy and "soak" in God's presence. These extended worship and ministry times allow members to listen, participate, and respond to the Holy Spirit in their midst. The sessions are aided by music, mood, and other

8. Moltmann, *Spirit of Life*, 35.

9. Cross, *People of God's Presence*, 7.

A POWERFUL PRESENCE

creative arts. The sacrament of communion and the practice of *lectio divina* can also help bring congregational members' attention to the mystical presence of Christ.[10] It is highly recommended that the extended worship sessions not replace the regular weekend services but occur in the evening or at other times and days, not to disrupt the regular rhythm of weekly worship. Jesus spoke of the wisdom in understanding the difference between "old and new wineskins" (Matt 9:17). The special worship sessions allow for greater spontaneity, freedom, experimentation, and responsiveness. Also, these extended worship sessions will benefit from the involvement of youth, young adults, and other non-clergy who typically do not lead. Indeed, these services often attract the youth and young adults. A Spirit-led experiment of soaking in God's presence allows God's people to rest and delight in God and watch him minister through the gifts to build up the body, thereby bringing renewed life to members.

2. Practice the Spiritual Gifts

The extended worship and ministry sessions allow congregational members to practice spiritual gifts, especially the "miraculous" gifts of faith, healing, miracles, prophecy, and words of knowledge. As members are filled with the Spirit in worship and praise, Jesus will prompt them to serve and build up his body through his gifts. In this way, the people of God's presence are a ministering community and royal priesthood. Serving others through spiritual gifts creates moments of divine resonance for people to encounter the living Christ. The atmosphere of worship and ministry creates a temple of the Holy Spirit where God is magnified and manifested. Men and women, boys and girls, clergy and non-clergy alike can participate in Christ's ministry to his body.

To support members in practicing spiritual gifts—especially the gift of prophecy—a Spirit-led experiment is for the church to host a workshop on prophetic ministry. A prophetic ministry

10. For more information on *lectio divina*, see, for example, Keating, *Intimacy with God*.

PROPOSALS FOR THE FUTURE: THE PENTECOSTAL ANGEL

workshop creates a safe environment for members to learn and grow in hearing and sharing prophetic words. Here members learn to hear and give prophetic words in a safe environment. They will also experience the joy of giving a timely prophetic word that resonates with others. Very few experiences measure up to the thrill of church members being used by God to serve and encourage others (Luke 10:17). Some helpful resources in this regard are Kris Vallotton's *Basic Training for the Prophetic Ministry*, Sam Storms's *Understanding Spiritual Gifts: A Comprehensive Guide*, and Havilah Cunnington's *Created to Hear God*.

3. Mission and the Spiritual Gifts

A third proposal is for churches to experiment in mission by sending members out on local outreaches utilizing the spiritual gifts, especially the power and vocal gifts of the Spirit. As Evangelicals are equipped with the gifts of faith, healing, miracles, prophecy, and words of knowledge, these ministries open opportunities for evangelism. These gifts create new pathways for evangelistic conversations, especially where some traditional efforts are no longer effective. Many North Americans today resist packaged messages or overly polished church services. However, God captures their attention when they experience a divine healing or prophetic word revealing the secrets of their hearts. The referent power of the Holy Spirit opens new channels of evangelism and authenticates the gospel's message. Divine resonance occurs when people experience emotional or physical healing or hear a prophetic word. The result of these encounters can lead nonbelievers to exclaim, "God is really among you!"

The biblical image for sending people out on local missions with divine power is Jesus sending out the Seventy (Luke 10:1-24). Not much is known about this group, but Luke describes them as "seventy others" since they were not a part of the original Twelve. Jesus enlists and empowers "seventy others" to drive out demons, cure diseases, heal the sick, and proclaim God's kingdom (9:1-2; 10:19). The Seventy's mission was so successful that, upon their return, Jesus exclaims, "I saw Satan fall like lightning from the heaven!" (10:18). When church members are equipped with all of the spiritual gifts, God uses them in extraordinary ways to communicate Christ's love and power.

4. Collaborate with Others

Churches hungry for God's presence can learn from other congregations with experience in the Spirit and spiritual gifts. Therefore, a fourth proposal is for churches to collaborate in worship, ministry, or mission with other Spirit-informed churches. For example, one Redding evangelical leader saw a place for Bethel to help them grow in supernatural ministry, like prophetic words, healing prayer, and deliverance ministry. I'm sure that this pastor and his church have areas that would aid and benefit Bethel, such as evangelism. It is a common truism that doctrine divides while mission unites. As churches partner together in ministry and mission—without compromising their own convictions—everyone grows. Collaborating in ministry opens congregational members to how others practice faith, which can add to new insights and learnings.

Another example of collaboration involved various churches in Redding. Several churches across denominations collaborated to hold an annual Good Friday service for the city. For the Good Friday services, no single church received credit or was named host. Instead they called themselves "the Church in Redding," and the collaboration paid off. By the tenth year of the Good Friday service, over seventy churches were participating with over ten thousand people in attendance! The Good Friday services were a big win for the kingdom and the city, and they allowed various congregations to serve alongside each other.

PROPOSALS FOR THE FUTURE: THE PENTECOSTAL ANGEL

5. The Challenge of Bethel Church

Bethel Church and neo-charismatic churches like it present a challenge to many evangelical churches locally and nationally. Attention to the Spirit's presence and referent power is something that many charismatic and Pentecostal churches bring to Christ's body in the age of modernity. However, despite their signs of life and renewal, there remain wells of the Spirit from which these congregations can draw new life. Lesslie Newbigin expresses concern about some forms of Pentecostalism, observing they sometimes isolate a particular truth at the expense of other important truths.[11] Newbigin's observation is helpful in three ways for Bethel's promising future.

First, culturally speaking, Bethel's direct and evidential spirituality creates a cavity for members to experience divine resonance. However, when emotions run high and turn into emotionalism, some members' spirituality becomes an escape from the immanent frame to emotionalism. Bethel is challenged to hold the tension between natural and supernatural, earthly and heavenly, the immanent and transcendent in their enthusiasm. As Root observes, life is found within the dialectic between life's given and non-given realities. Second, Bethel holds a robust understanding of the Spirit as the divine *ruach* of life. However, as Moltmann observes, the work of the Spirit always has the work of Christ as its goal. Therefore, Bethel is challenged to hold together a Trinitarian framework in occasions of heightened spiritual enthusiasm. Bethel would be well served to keep the Spirit *of Christ* central in its experience of Spirit. By keeping Christ the focus of its spiritual enthusiasm, Bethel members' spirituality will lead to Christoformity. Here, the experience of the Spirit leads to their transformation "into the image of the Son" (Rom 8:29). Third and finally, Bethel rightly affirms the biblical view of the Spirit's advent and God's numinous power in the church. However, Bethel is challenged to keep the eschatological horizon of Jesus's return in view, especially in its healing ministry. Understanding healing

11. Newbigin, *Household of God*, 127.

A POWERFUL PRESENCE

ministry as a present but also partial, provisional, or ambiguous reality, will lead members to find grace and the Spirit's comfort in unrealized prayer. As the apostle Paul declares, God's grace is sufficient, even in our times of weakness.

Sermon Series in 1 and 2 Corinthians

Considering these challenges, a proposal for Bethel is to journey through a three-month sermon series on "God's Power in Weakness" from 1 and 2 Corinthians. A study of the Corinthian correspondences is fitting, considering the Corinthians' charismatic character and enthusiasm for the Spirit. In 1 and 2 Corinthians, Paul underscores the Spirit's presence and power in human weakness. Paul also rightly affirms God's commitment to transform our "lowly" bodies (1 Cor 15:35–57). A sermon series in 1 and 2 Corinthians would direct Bethel members toward the joy of the Spirit in patient endurance (1 Cor 15:58).

This three-month sermon series on "God's Power in Weakness" in 1 and 2 Corinthians would be aided by testimonies from congregational members with physical and developmental disabilities. Personal stories of faith and endurance from people and family members affected by physical and developmental disabilities would testify to God's goodness and power despite human weakness. These testimonies would be powerful reminders of God's action amid unanswered prayer. Testimonies from these community members exemplify persevering faith, hope, and love.

Not coincidentally, I experienced such a worship service during my time at Bethel. Specifically, my family and I participated in a Bethel monthly worship service specifically designed for people and family members with developmental and cognitive disabilities. Called "Intimacy with the King," the people involved in these services were affected by visible and non-visible challenges, such as autism, genetic abnormalities, and cognitive disabilities. My wife, family, and I participated along with our son, Garrett, who was born with Down syndrome, mentioned in the preface. Garrett, now twenty years old, enjoyed these gatherings at Bethel,

120

where he worshipped and served along with other people with disabilities. The worship services were a beautiful picture of God's goodness and power at Bethel Church. As Bethel extends these testimonies to the broader congregation, they will highlight God's powerful presence in human weakness.

Chapter 7

Conclusion: Word and Spirit

Word and Spirit together, canonical language and the Spirit of life, are the joint bearers of that unique culture of the kingdom of God that entered the world in Jesus Christ.—Kevin Vanhoozer, *The Drama of Doctrine*

In Matt 22, the Sadducees propose a question to Jesus, intending to discredit the Galilean and his ministry. The Sadducees, who do not believe in a resurrection of the dead, the afterlife, or that God continued to speak to his people following Moses, present Jesus with a ridiculous scenario to protect their socially privileged position. In the scenario, a married man dies without having children, and the man's widow subsequently marries his six other brothers—one after another—who then also die without having any children. Thinking they have trapped Jesus with their theological predicament, the Sadducees lay their final blow. They ask, "Now then, at the resurrection, whose wife will she be of the seven, since all of them were married to her?" (v. 28). Jesus responds in a way that exposes the deficiency of the Sadducees' faith. "Jesus replied, 'You are in error because you do not know the Scriptures or the power of God'" (v. 29).

CONCLUSION: WORD AND SPIRIT

Some Christians today suffer from the same deficiency as the Sadducees. Although they may not share the Sadducees' agnosticism toward the resurrection and afterlife, some modern Christians fail to know the Scriptures or the power of God. According to Jesus, one must know *both*—the Scriptures and the power of God—to see God and understand his action in the world. It is not enough to have one without the other—the Scriptures or the power of God—but one needs both to discern his work in a location. Knowing the Scripture without the power of God leads to an anemic faith. Knowing the power of God without the Scripture leads to a faith adrift. The church of Christ, however, lives by word *and* Spirit. Abiding in word *and* Spirit empowers the church to properly worship God and discern his work in new settings (John 4:24).[1] And only word and Spirit can adequately lead the church into its bright and promising future (1 Pet 1:23; John 3:5–8).

In this vein, the rise of neo-charismatic Christianity is a Spirit disruption. God is at work within charismatic/Pentecostal faith, creating a cavity inside a modern church that has accommodated the reductions of the immanent frame. What the Spirit is doing is contextual. He's pouring his supernatural power upon an anemic church languishing in the malaise of immanence. God has unleashed his Spirit to manifest Christ's supernatural presence and power in his people for the world. This Spirit disruption stimulates the church to reimagine God's action today. God seeks to pour out his numinous power upon his church, which desperately needs *life*—vibrant, sustaining, abundant life. As the apostle Paul reminds the Thessalonians, the gospel comes in word *and* power (1 Thess 1:5).

In response to the Spirit's disruption, God calls the church to walk forward in boldness of humility and faith. Like the prophet Ezekiel, God calls the church to prophesy and breathe new life into a valley of dry bones (37:4). Ezekiel prayed, "O dry bones, hear the word of the Lord. . . . Behold, I will cause breath to enter

---

1. Others have artfully stated it: "All word and no Spirit, we dry up; all Spirit and no word, we blow up; both word and Spirit, we grow up."

A POWERFUL PRESENCE

you, and you shall live" (v. 5). Today God is enlisting prophetic leaders to breathe new life again into his people. As the church moves forward in faith and Spirit, it cooperates in Jesus's supernatural ministry. Jesus has conferred his ministry to the church in the power of the Spirit. The church is called to "heal the sick, raise the dead, cleanse those who have leprosy, [and] drive out demons" (Matt 10:8). The church must resist the temptation to secure life through the expenditure of energy in the hopes of accumulating resource or relevance. As Jesus himself said, "For whoever wants to save his life will lose it, but whoever loses his life for me, will find it" (Matt 16:25). Therefore, as the church worships, rests, prays, waits, and ministers in the power of the Spirit, God will breathe new life again into Christ's church to manifest his powerful presence in the world (Luke 24:49).

Appendix

Bethel's Responses to Questions and Concerns

THE FOLLOWING ARE RESPONSES and resources from Bethel Church addressing questions and concerns regarding their beliefs and practices. They are offered here for readers who wish to explore some of Bethel's positions on controversial issues further. As mentioned, the purpose of this book is not to problem solve or offer a defense or critique of Bethel. Rather, this present work is an appreciative inquiry based on ethnographic data exploring Bethel's understanding and use of supernatural power. In observing, participating, and interviewing at Bethel, I considered the church to affirm and practice historic, Trinitarian, and orthodox Christian faith within the charismatic/Pentecostal stream. However, as I have indicated in this book, there were places where I believe Bethel is challenged to find resurrected life in Christ in the power of the Holy Spirit culturally, theologically, and biblically. Therefore, I approached Bethel pastorally, not defensively or critically.

My approach to understanding all faith communities, Bethel included, reflects Mark Baker's understanding of a centered-set church. Drawing upon the work of anthropologist Paul Hiebert, Baker presents the concepts of "bounded," "fuzzy," and "centered" Christian communities to describe how churches understand themselves and relate to others. Bounded churches are defined by

125

APPENDIX: BETHEL'S RESPONSES TO QUESTIONS AND CONCERNS

the lines they draw. Baker writes, "Bounded churches draw a line that distinguishes insiders from outsiders, Christians from non-Christians, or true Christians from mediocre Christians."[1] These lines involve correct beliefs and specific visible behaviors and practices. Baker observes, "[While] lines provide clear guidance, they can also hinder us from hearing the Spirit's call."[2] Bounded communities can lead to forms of judgmentalism and conditional love. Fuzzy churches seek to avoid the problems associated with bounded churches by erasing the lines. Fuzzy churches define themselves, saying, "No more lines!" However, fuzzy churches operate from the same line-/non-line-drawing construct as bounded churches. Fuzzy churches can also suffer from relativism, a lack of discipleship, and leading people directionless. Over time, tolerance, virtue signaling, and group think/uniformity become supreme values in fuzzy churches. Centered-set churches operate from a different paradigm from bounded and fuzzy churches. Centered churches discern membership through people's direction and relationship to the center, which is Christ. A centered church still has a place for conversion, repentance, doctrine, and discipleship because it is founded upon one's general orientation and movement toward God in Christ in the fellowship of the Spirit. With centered churches, "the line does not define the person's relationship to the group. Rather, the line emerges by observing a person's relationship with the center."[3] The centered-set paradigm helps congregations live by the Spirit, bear the fruit of the Spirit, and avoid judgmentalism and relativism. The *Spirit* keeps centered churches together, not lines, power moves, or fuzzy tolerance. Baker's centered-set concept sheds light on how Christians and Christian communities like Bethel operate within broader evangelicalism.

Considering Baker's concept of centered-set churches, the following is a list of resources from Bethel Church concerning questions about the church.

1. Baker, *Centered-Set Church*, 24.
2. Baker, *Centered-Set Church*, 3.
3. Baker, *Centered-Set Church*, 28.

APPENDIX: BETHEL'S RESPONSES TO QUESTIONS AND CONCERNS

Bethel's statement of faith can be found on their website: https://www.bethel.com/beliefs#statement-of-faith.

Bethel's *Rediscover Bethel* series on YouTube addresses several of the church's beliefs and practices, such as:

- On the Trinity, Jesus as "perfect theology," theology of sickness and healing, and use of the Passion Translation, *Rediscover Bethel*, episode 1, https://www.youtube.com/watch?v=XZ2xjnXYfm8&list=PLUaRlPOu98poclsGoUojGoU91tl5q3-sK&index=1

- On Christology, preaching and faith, and theology of sickness, *Rediscover Bethel*, episode 2, https://www.youtube.com/watch?v=w2vRRZwN1Wg&list=PLUaRlPOu98poclsGoUojGoU91tl5q3-sK&index=2

- On grave sucking/soaking, physical manifestations, kundalini spirit, holy laughter, and glory clouds, *Rediscover Bethel*, episode 3, https://www.youtube.com/watch?v=3c7s-WCKIrQ&list=PLUaRlPOu98poclsGoUojGoU91tl5q3-sK&index=3

- On fivefold ministry, denominations, New Apostolic Reformation, and Seven Mountain Mandate and dominionism, *Rediscover Bethel*, episode 4, https://www.youtube.com/watch?v=TVAVfD5OSkU&list=PLUaRlPOu98poclsGoUojGoU91tl5q3-sK&index=4

- On prophecy, prophets, false prophets, prophetic risk, and the prosperity gospel, *Rediscover Bethel*, episode 5, https://www.youtube.com/watch?v=CuKoxpb43RU&list=PLUaRlPOu98poclsGoUojGoU91tl5q3-sK&index=5

- On Bill Johnson on apostleship, Seven-Mountain dominionism, Bethel being a cult (?), and politics, *Rediscover Bethel*, episode 6, https://www.youtube.com/watch?v=a8NIyedUex8&list=PLUaRlPOu98poclsGoUojGoU91tl5q3-sK&index=6

Bethel understands their practice of physical manifestations as consistent with manifestations with previous revivals:

APPENDIX: BETHEL'S RESPONSES TO QUESTIONS AND CONCERNS

http://pneumareview.com/supernatural-physical-manifestations-pking/.

- From Bethel's "Revival Apologetics" course regarding John Wesley's ministry and supernatural manifestations: "There were, of course, many factors of Wesley's ministry and message that caused both excitement and anxiety. No small aspect of the controversy included the seemingly routine scene of people weeping, violently shaking, crying out, losing consciousness, falling down, and occasionally becoming uncontrollably agitated during his meetings. Manifestations were often dismissed by detractors as 'enthusiasm.'"[4]

- On A. B. Simpson, founder of the Christian and Missionary Alliance and revival manifestations: "In 1897 A. B. Simpson wrote that one of the effects of being filled with the spirit is the 'fullness of joy so that the heart is constantly radiant. This does not depend on circumstances, it fills the spirit with holy laughter in the midst of the most trying surroundings.' Simpson himself records in his diary on September 12 1907, that he experienced holy laughter for more than an hour."[5]

- From Oswald Chambers's journal regarding holy laughter: "It is an unspeakably blessed thing to see souls come out under the blessing of the baptism of the Holy Ghost and fire. Some simply laugh, peels of the heartiest and most blessed laughter you've ever heard, just a modern addition of then was our mouth filled with laughter." Chambers also writes, "Many souls cut loose, there were tears and laughter and all the blessed signs of those revival times the Lord brings so mysteriously and suddenly upon his people. It is a great business to open up all the windows of the soul to heaven and live on the Hallelujah side."[6]

---

4. Beard, *Thunderstruck*.
5. Nienkirchen, *A. B. Simpson*, 145.
6. Chambers, *Oswald Chambers*, 104–5.

Bibliography

Baker, Mark. *Centered-Set Church: Discipleship and Community Without Judgmentalism.* Downers Grove, IL: IVP Academic, 2021.

Barnes, Roscoe. F. F. *Bosworth: The Man Behind "Christ the Healer."* Newcastle, Eng.: Cambridge Scholars, 2009.

Beard, Steven. *Thunderstruck: John Wesley and the "Toronto Blessing."* Wilmore, KY: Thunderstruck, 1996.

Bebbington, D. W. *Evangelism in Modern Britain: A History from the 1730s to the 1980s.* New York: Unwin Hyman, 2002.

Bethel. *Rediscover Bethel.* Episode 4, "The Church, Ministry, and the New Apostolic Reformation." YouTube, June 30, 2021. https://www.youtube.com/watch?v=TVAVfD5OSkU&t=2877s.

Bevans, Stephan B. *Models of Contextual Theology.* Maryknoll, NY: Orbis, 1992.

Bevans, Stephan B., and Roger P. Schroeder. *Prophetic Dialogue: Reflections on Christian Mission Today.* Maryknoll, NY: Orbis, 2011.

Blue, Ken. *Authority to Heal: Answers for Everyone Who Has Prayed for a Sick Friend.* Downers Grove, IL: InterVarsity, 1987.

Branson, Mark Lau. *Memories, Hopes, and Conversations: Appreciative Inquiry, Missional Engagement, and Congregational Change.* 2nd ed. Lanham, MD: Rowman & Littlefield, 2016.

BroadStreet. *The Passion Translation: The New Testament with Psalms, Proverbs, and Song of Songs.* 2nd ed. Savage, MN: BroadStreet, 2018.

Brown, Jeannine K. *Scripture as Communication: Introducing Biblical Hermeneutics.* Grand Rapids: Baker Academic, 2007.

Burgess, Stanley M., and Eduard van der Maas, eds. *The New International Dictionary of Pentecostal and Charismatic Movements.* Rev. ed. Grand Rapids: Zondervan, 2022.

Bush, Andrew F., and Carolyn C. Wason. *Millennials and the Mission of God: A Prophetic Dialogue.* Eugene, OR: Wipf & Stock, 2017.

Chambers, Bertha. *Oswald Chambers: His Life and Work.* London: Simpkin Marshall, 1947.

BIBLIOGRAPHY

Christina BRSLO. "False Prophesies Mixed with Kundalini at Bill Johnson's Bethel Redding Church." YouTube, May 14, 2017. https://www.youtube.com/watch?v=T20gYvSRlWU.

Cross, Terry L. *The People of God's Presence: An Introduction to Ecclesiology.* Grand Rapids: Baker Academic, 2019.

———. *Serving the People of God's Presence: A Theology of Ministry.* Grand Rapids: Baker Academic, 2020.

Cunnington, Havilah. *Created to Hear God: 4 Unique and Proven Ways to Confidently Discern His Voice.* Nashville: Nelson, 2023.

Davis, Jim, et al. *The Great Dechurching: Who's Leaving, Why Are They Going, and What Will It Take to Bring Them Back?* Grand Rapids: Zondervan, 2023.

Dunn, James D. G. *Baptism in the Spirit: A Re-Examination of the New Testament Teaching on the Gift of the Spirit in Relation to Pentecostalism Today.* London: SCM, 2010.

———. *Jesus and the Spirit: A Study of the Religious and Charismatic Experience of Jesus and the First Christians as Reflected in the New Testament.* Grand Rapids: Eerdmans, 1997.

———. *Unity and Diversity in the New Testament: An Inquiry into the Character of Earliest Christianity.* 2nd ed. Harrisburg, PA: Trinity International, 1990.

Ellingworth, P. "Priests." In *New Dictionary of Biblical Theology: Exploring the Unity & Diversity of Scripture,* edited by T. Desmond Alexander and Brian S. Rosner. IVP Reference Collection. Downers Grove, IL: InterVarsity, 2000. Accordance software ed.

Emerson, Robert M., et al. *Writing Ethnographic Fieldnotes.* Chicago: University of Chicago Press, 1995.

Erickson, Millard J. *Introducing Christian Doctrine.* Grand Rapids: Baker, 1992.

Farrelly, Dann. "Revivalist Lifestyle." Handout, Bethel School of Supernatural Ministry, Nov. 21, 2022.

Fee, Gordon D. *The Disease of Health and Wealth Gospels.* Costa Mesa, CA: Word for Today, 1979.

———. *The First Epistle to the Corinthians.* New International Commentary on the New Testament. Grand Rapids: Eerdmans, 2014.

———. *God's Empowering Presence: The Holy Spirit in the Letters of Paul.* Peabody, MA: Hendrickson, 1994.

Fitch, David E. *Faithful Presence: Seven Disciplines That Shape the Church for Mission.* Downers Grove, IL: IVP, 2016.

Francis, Jermaine, and Rebecca Francis. *Activating the Gift of Prophecy: Your Guide to Receiving and Sharing what God is Saying.* Shippensburg, PA: Destiny Image, 2019.

Fuller, David Otis, ed. *Spurgeon's Lectures to His Students.* Grand Rapids: Zondervan, 1945.

Gombis, Timothy G. *Power in Weakness: Paul's Transformed Vision for Ministry.* Grand Rapids: Eerdmans, 2021.

Gorman, Michael J. *Cruciformity: Paul's Narrative Spirituality of the Cross.* Grand Rapids: Eerdmans, 2001.

BIBLIOGRAPHY

Grudem, Wayne. *Systematic Theology: An Introduction to Biblical Doctrine.* Grand Rapids: Zondervan, 1994.

Guder, Darrell L., ed. *Missional Church: A Vision for the Sending of the Church in North America.* Grand Rapids: Eerdmans, 1998.

Hawthorne, Gerald E. *The Presence and the Power: The Significance of the Holy Spirit in the Life and Ministry of Jesus.* Dallas: Word, 1991.

Hays, Richard B. *The Moral Vision of the New Testament: Community, Cross, New Creation; A Contemporary Introduction to New Testament Ethics.* New York: HarperCollins, 1996.

Holland, Joe, and Peter Henriot. *Social Analysis: Linking Faith and Justice.* Maryknoll, NY: Orbis, 1984.

Horn, David, and Gordon L. Isaac, eds. *Great Awakenings: Historical Perspectives for Today.* Peabody: Hendrickson, 2016.

Johnson, Bill. *Defining Moments: God-Encounters with Ordinary People Who Changed the World.* New Kensington, PA: Whitaker, 2016.

———. *Experience the Impossible: Simple Ways to Unleash Heaven's Power on Earth.* Minneapolis: Chosen, 2014.

———. *Face to Face with God.* Lake Mary, FL: Charisma, 2015.

———. "The Gospel only comes in one form—one that transforms lives." Facebook, Oct. 24, 2022. https://www.facebook.com/BillJohnsonMinistries/posts/pfbid02bwe1DzTj2qXd35xGR7wy6WHaPfFXvD836VndWnGg6G58s6eTFGq2oD4rGCWMoUp1l.

———. *Hosting the Presence: Unveiling Heaven's Agenda.* Shippensburg, PA: Destiny Image, 2012.

———. "Receiving and Walking in the Power of the Holy Spirit: Bill Johnson Sermon, Bethel Church." YouTube, June 4, 2023. https://www.youtube.com/watch?v=SnxNzFtX_wE.

———. *When Heaven Invades Earth: A Practical Guide to a Life of Miracles.* Shippensburg, PA: Destiny Image, 2013.

Jones, Martyn Wendell. "Inside the Popular, Controversial Bethel Church." *Christianity Today*, May 2016. https://www.christianitytoday.com/2016/04/cover-story-inside-popular-controversial-bethel-church/.

Keating, Thomas. *Intimacy with God.* New York: Crossroad, 1994.

Keener, Craig S. *1–2 Corinthians.* New Cambridge Bible Commentary. New York: Cambridge University Press, 2005.

———. *Acts: An Exegetical Commentary.* 4 vols. Grand Rapids: Baker Academic, 2012.

Kraft, Charles H. *Christianity in Culture: A Study in Biblical Theologizing in Cross-Cultural Perspective.* Maryknoll, NY: Orbis, 2005.

———. *Issues in Contextualization.* Pasadena: Carey Library, 2016.

King, Paul L. *Genuine Gold: The Cautiously Charismatic Story of the Early Christian and Missionary Alliance.* Tulsa: Word & Spirit, 2006.

———. *Nuggets of Gold: Simpson, Tozer, Jaffray, and Other Christian & Missionary Alliance Leaders on Experiencing the Spirit-Empowered Life.* Tulsa: Word & Spirit, 2010.

BIBLIOGRAPHY

Kosmin, Barry A., et al. *American Nones: The Profile of the No Religion Population; A Report Based on the American Religious Identification Survey 2008*. Hartford: Program on Public Values [Trinity College], 2009. https://commons.trincoll.edu/aris/files/2011/08/NONES_08.pdf.

Liardon, Roberts. *God's Generals: Why They Succeeded and Why Some Failed*. New Kensington, PA: Whitaker, 1996.

Lofland, John, and Lyn H. Lofland. *Analyzing Social Settings: A Guide to Qualitative Observation and Analysis*. Belmont, CA: Wadsworth, 1995.

MacArthur, John. *Strange Fire: The Danger of Offending the Holy Spirit with Counterfeit Worship*. Nashville: Nelson, 2013.

Markofski, Wes. *New Monasticism and the Transformation of American Evangelicalism*. New York: Oxford University Press, 2015.

McKnight, Scot. *Pastor Paul: Nurturing a Culture of Christoformity in the Church*. Theological Exploration for the Church Catholic. Grand Rapids: Brazos, 2019.

McLoughlin, William G., Jr. *Modern Revivalism: Charles Grandison Finney to Billy Graham*. Eugene, OR: Wipf & Stock, 2004.

McLoughlin, William G. *Revivals, Awakenings, and Reform*. Chicago: University of Chicago Press, 1978.

Migliore, Daniel L. *Faith Seeking Understanding: An Introduction to Christian Theology*. Grand Rapids: Eerdmans, 1991.

Moltmann, Jürgen. *The Church in the Power of the Spirit: A Contribution to Messianic Ecclesiology*. San Francisco: Harper & Row, 1977.

———. *God in Creation: A New Theology of Creation and the Spirit of God*. London: SCM, 1985.

———. *History and the Triune God: Contributions to Trinitarian Theology*. London: SCM, 1991.

———. *The Source of Life: The Holy Spirit and the Theology of Life*. London: SCM, 1997.

———. *The Spirit of Life: A Universal Affirmation*. Minneapolis: Fortress, 1993.

Moschella, Mary Clark. *Ethnography as a Pastoral Practice: An Introduction*. Cleveland: Pilgrim, 2008.

Newbigin, Lesslie. *The Gospel in a Pluralist Society*. Grand Rapids: Eerdmans, 1989.

———. *The Household of God*. Carlisle, Eng.: Paternoster, 1998.

———. *A Word in Season: Perspectives on Christian World Missions*. Grand Rapids: Eerdmans, 1994.

Nienkirchen, Charles W. *A. B. Simpson and the Pentecostal Movement*. Peabody, MA: Hendrickson, 1992.

Nieuwhof, Carey. "5 Reasons Charismatic Churches Are Growing." Carey Nieuwhof, n.d. https://careynieuwhof.com/5-reasons-charismatic-churches-are-growing-and-attractional-churches-are-past-peak/.

Pinnock, Clark H. *Flame of Love: A Theology of the Holy Spirit*. Downers Grove, IL: IVP Academic, 1996.

BIBLIOGRAPHY

Pivec, Holly, and Douglas R. Geivett. *Counterfeit Kingdom: The Dangers of New Revelation, New Prophets, and New Age Practices in the Church.* Nashville: B&H, 2022.

Poloma, Margaret M. "The Toronto Blessing." In *The New International Dictionary of Pentecostal and Charismatic Movements*, edited by Stanley M. Burgess and Eduard van der Maas, 1149–52. Rev. ed. Grand Rapids: Zondervan, 2022

Root, Andrew. *Churches and the Crisis of Decline: A Hopeful, Practical Ecclesiology for a Secular Age.* Grand Rapids: Baker Academic, 2022.

————. *The Congregation in a Secular Age: Keeping Sacred Time Against the Speed of Modern Life.* Grand Rapids: Baker Academic, 2021.

————. *Faith Formation in a Secular Age: Responding to the Church's Obsession with Youthfulness.* Grand Rapids: Baker Academic, 2017.

————. *The Pastor in a Secular Age: Ministry to People Who No Longer Need God.* Grand Rapids: Baker Academic, 2021.

Rosa, Hartmut. *Resonance: A Sociology of Our Relationship to the World.* Cambridge: Polity, 2019.

Roxburgh, Alan J. *Joining God, Remaking the Church, Changing the World: The New Shape of the Church in Our Time.* New York: Morehouse, 2015.

————. *Structured for Mission: Renewing the Culture of the Church.* Downers Grove, IL: IVP 2015.

Roxburgh, Alan J., and Martin Robinson. *Practices for the Refounding of God's People: The Missional Challenge of the West.* New York: Church, 2018.

Ryken, Leland, et al., eds. "Church." *Dictionary of Biblical Imagery.* Downers Grove, IL: InterVarsity, 1998.

Scharen, Christian B. *Explorations in Ecclesiology and Ethnography.* Grand Rapids: Eerdmans, 2012.

Schreiter, Robert J., ed. *Constructing Local Theologies.* Maryknoll, NY: Orbis, 2003.

Schultz, Thom. "The Rise of the Dones: The 'Done With Church' Population." *Church Leaders*, Jan. 28, 2020. https://churchleaders.com/outreach-missions/outreach-missions-articles/177144-thom-schultz-rise-of-the-done-with-church-population.html.

Sine, Tom. *The Mustard Seed Conspiracy: You Can Make a Difference in the World.* Waco: Word, 1981.

Smith, James K. A. *How (Not) To be Secular: Reading Charles Taylor.* Grand Rapids: Eerdmans, 2014.

Springer, Kevin, and John Wimber. *Power Evangelism.* San Francisco: Harper & Row, 1986.

Stackhouse, John G. *Evangelicalism: A Very Short Introduction.* Very Short Introductions. New York: Oxford University Press, 2022.

Stackhouse, Max L. *Apologia: Contextualization, Globalization and Mission in Theological Education.* Grand Rapids: Eerdmans, 1988.

Steinke, Peter L. *A Door Set Open: Grounding Change in Mission and Hope.* Herndon, VA: Alban Institute, 2010.

BIBLIOGRAPHY

Stetzer, Ed. "Pentecostals: How Do They Keep Growing While Other Groups Are Declining?" *Church Leaders*, June 27, 2023. https://churchleaders.com/voices/453879-pentecostals-how-do-they-keep-growing.html.

Stewart, James S. *A Man in Christ*. London: Hodder & Stoughton, 1935.

Storms, Sam. *Understanding Spiritual Gifts: A Comprehensive Guide*. Grand Rapids: Zondervan, 2020.

Taylor, Charles. *A Secular Age*. Cambridge, MA: Belknap, 2007.

Taylor, John V. *The Go-Between God: The Holy Spirit and the Christian Mission*. New York: Oxford University Press, 1979.

Thiselton, Anthony C. *The First Epistle to the Corinthians*. New International Greek New Testament Commentary. Grand Rapids: Eerdmans, 2000.

Tickle, Phyllis, with Jon M. Sweeney. *The Age of the Spirit: How the Ghost of an Ancient Controversy Is Shaping the Church*. Grand Rapids: Baker, 2014.

Tozer, A. W. *The Knowledge of the Holy*. San Francisco: HarperOne, 1978.

———. *The Pursuit of God*. Mansfield, CT: Martino, 2009.

U.S. Immigrations and Customs Enforcement. *SEVIS by the Numbers: Annual Report on International Student Trends*. Department of Homeland Security, 2022. https://www.dhs.gov/sites/default/files/2024-05/22_0406_hsi_sevp-cy22-sevis-btn.pdf.

Vallotton, Kris. *Basic Training for the Prophetic Ministry*. Rev. ed. Shippensburg, PA: Destiny Image, 2014.

———. *Developing a Supernatural Lifestyle: A Practical Guide to a Life of Signs, Wonders, and Miracles*. Shippensburg, PA: Destiny Image, 2007.

Van Engen, Charles. *God's Missionary People: Rethinking the Purpose of the Local Church*. Grand Rapids: Baker, 1991.

Vanhoozer, Kevin L. *The Drama of Doctrine: A Canonical-Linguistic Approach to Christian Theology*. Louisville: Westminster John Knox, 2005.

Vine, W. E., et al., eds. *Vine's Expository Dictionary of Biblical Words*. Nashville: Nelson, 1985.

Wagner, C. Peter. *Churchquake: How the New Apostolic Reformation Is Shaking Up the Church As We Know It*. Raleigh: Regal, 1999.

Walls, Andrew. *The Missionary Movement in Christian History: Studies in the Transmission of Faith*. Maryknoll, NY: Orbis, 1996.

Well, Samuel. *A Future That's Bigger than the Past: Catalysing Kingdom Communities*. London: Canterbury Norwich, 2019.

White, James E. *The Rise of the Nones: Understanding and Reaching the Religiously Unaffiliated*. Grand Rapids: Baker, 2014.

Willard, Dallas. *Hearing God: Developing a Conversational Relationship with God*. Downers Grove, IL: InterVarsity, 1999.

Yancey, George. "Who's More Political: Progressive or Conservative Christians?" *Gospel Coalition*, Apr. 29, 2021. https://www.thegospelcoalition.org/article/political-progressive-conservative-christians/.

Zahl, Simeon. *The Holy Spirit and Christian Experience*. London: Oxford University Press, 2020.

www.ingramcontent.com/pod-product-compliance
Lightning Source LLC
LaVergne TN
LVHW021252070125
800704LV00023B/236